# Lecture Notes in Computer Science 16214

Founding Editors

Gerhard Goos
Juris Hartmanis

Editorial Board Members

Elisa Bertino, *Purdue University, West Lafayette, IN, USA*
Wen Gao, *Peking University, Beijing, China*
Bernhard Steffen, *TU Dortmund University, Dortmund, Germany*
Moti Yung, *Columbia University, New York, NY, USA*

The series Lecture Notes in Computer Science (LNCS), including its subseries Lecture Notes in Artificial Intelligence (LNAI) and Lecture Notes in Bioinformatics (LNBI), has established itself as a medium for the publication of new developments in computer science and information technology research, teaching, and education.

LNCS enjoys close cooperation with the computer science R & D community, the series counts many renowned academics among its volume editors and paper authors, and collaborates with prestigious societies. Its mission is to serve this international community by providing an invaluable service, mainly focused on the publication of conference and workshop proceedings and postproceedings. LNCS commenced publication in 1973.

Xiaoqing Guo · Yueming Jin · Hala Lamdouar ·
Qianhui Men · Cheng Ouyang · Manish Sahu ·
S. Swaroop Vedula
Editors

# Human-AI Collaboration

First International Workshop, HAIC 2025
Held in Conjunction with MICCAI 2025
Daejeon, South Korea, September 27, 2025
Proceedings

*Editors*
Xiaoqing Guo
Hong Kong Baptist University
Hong Kong, China

Yueming Jin
National University of Singapore
Singapore, Singapore

Hala Lamdouar
University of Oxford
Oxford, UK

Qianhui Men
University of Bristol
Bristol, UK

Cheng Ouyang
University of Oxford
Oxford, UK

Manish Sahu
Johns Hopkins University
Baltimore, MD, USA

S. Swaroop Vedula
Johns Hopkins University
Baltimore, MD, USA

ISSN 0302-9743 ISSN 1611-3349 (electronic)
Lecture Notes in Computer Science
ISBN 978-3-032-08969-4 ISBN 978-3-032-08970-0 (eBook)
https://doi.org/10.1007/978-3-032-08970-0

© The Editor(s) (if applicable) and The Author(s), under exclusive license to Springer Nature Switzerland AG 2026

This work is subject to copyright. All rights are solely and exclusively licensed by the Publisher, whether the whole or part of the material is concerned, specifically the rights of translation, reprinting, reuse of illustrations, recitation, broadcasting, reproduction on microfilms or in any other physical way, and transmission or information storage and retrieval, electronic adaptation, computer software, or by similar or dissimilar methodology now known or hereafter developed.
The use of general descriptive names, registered names, trademarks, service marks, etc. in this publication does not imply, even in the absence of a specific statement, that such names are exempt from the relevant protective laws and regulations and therefore free for general use.
The publisher, the authors and the editors are safe to assume that the advice and information in this book are believed to be true and accurate at the date of publication. Neither the publisher nor the authors or the editors give a warranty, expressed or implied, with respect to the material contained herein or for any errors or omissions that may have been made. The publisher remains neutral with regard to jurisdictional claims in published maps and institutional affiliations.

This Springer imprint is published by the registered company Springer Nature Switzerland AG
The registered company address is: Gewerbestrasse 11, 6330 Cham, Switzerland

If disposing of this product, please recycle the paper.

# Preface

The First MICCAI Workshop on Human-AI Collaboration (HAIC 2025) was held on September 27, 2025, in conjunction with the 28th International Conference on Medical Imaging and Computer-Assisted Intervention (MICCAI 2025).

The success of artificial intelligence in dynamic real-world healthcare environments necessitates effective collaborations with human experts. Despite the rapidly advancing capabilities of AI in MIC and CAI, there is an unmet need for a systematic framing and discussion on topics centred on human-AI collaboration.

The HAIC 2025 workshop offered the first systematic discussion forum addressing all aspects of human-AI collaboration for the MICCAI community. We aimed to raise awareness about human-AI collaboration in MIC and CAI and spark discussions on identifying and addressing frequently overlooked challenges that involve human factors. The workshop complemented existing topics in MICCAI and its satellite events, and ultimately brought unique value to both research and clinical practice.

The proceedings of HAIC 2025 include 9 high-quality papers selected among 12 submissions through a double-blind peer review process, with most submissions reviewed by at least 3 reviewers among a Program Committee of 22 experts covering diverse expertise, and further meta-reviewed by at least 2 Organization Committee members. The accepted works cover multiple key areas on HAIC in the context of MICCAI, including but are not limited to human-in-the-loop model training, design and assessment for human-AI joint systems and workflows, interactive environments for clinical training, and enhancing transparency and trustworthiness for joint systems. These submissions are grounded on a comprehensive spectrum of clinical scenarios, including supporting tumor diagnosis, re-examining interpretability approaches in real-world contexts, modeling inter-observer variability among different expertise levels, and enhancing human skills during surgical interventions, among others.

The scientific program featured keynote talks from academia, clinical practice, and industry, alongside high-quality oral and spotlight presentations. We sincerely thank the speakers for their insightful presentations, all authors for their excellent contributions, and the Program Committee for their rigorous and thoughtful reviews. We are also deeply grateful for the generous support provided by the Advisory Committee: Qi Dou, Helen Higham, Nassir Navab, and Alison Noble. Special thanks to Stephen Aylward, Daguang

Xu, and their teams, representing NVIDIA Corporation, for organizing their generous sponsorship and delivering an insightful industry talk.

September 2025

Xiaoqing Guo
Yueming Jin
Hala Lamdouar
Qianhui Men
Cheng Ouyang
Manish Sahu
S. Swaroop Vedula

# Organization

## Organization Committee

| | |
|---|---|
| Xiaoqing Guo | Hong Kong Baptist University, China |
| Yueming Jin | National University of Singapore, Singapore |
| Hala Lamdouar | University of Oxford, UK |
| Qianhui Men | University of Bristol, UK |
| Cheng Ouyang | University of Oxford, UK |
| Manish Sahu | Johns Hopkins University, USA |
| S. Swaroop Vedula | Johns Hopkins University, USA |

## Advisory Board

| | |
|---|---|
| Qi Dou | Chinese University of Hong Kong, China |
| Helen Higham | University of Oxford, UK |
| Nassir Navab | Technical University of Munich, Germany |
| Alison Noble | University of Oxford, UK |

## Program Committee

| | |
|---|---|
| Alex Moehring | Purdue University, USA |
| Bernhard Kainz | FAU Erlangen-Nürnberg, Germany & Imperial College London, UK |
| Caroline Essert | Université de Strasbourg, France |
| David Black | University of British Columbia, Canada |
| Francis Xiatian Zhang | University of Edinburgh, UK |
| Haojun Jiang | Tsinghua University, China |
| Harry Rogers | University of Oxford, UK |
| Hermione Warr | University of Oxford, UK |
| Jiancheng Yang | École Polytechnique Fédérale de Lausanne, Switzerland |
| Kun Yuan | University of Strasbourg, France |
| Linlin Shen | Shenzhen University, China |
| Mohammad Alsharid | Khalifa University, UAE |
| Muhammad Ridzuan | Mohamed bin Zayed University of Artificial Intelligence, UAE |

| | |
|---|---|
| Qian Li | National University of Singapore, Singapore |
| Qiaoyu Zheng | Shanghai Jiao Tong University, China |
| Runlong He | University College London, UK |
| Ruoyu Chen | Institute of Information Engineering, Chinese Academy of Sciences, China |
| Ryo Fujii | Keio University, Japan |
| Yasin Ibrahim | University of Oxford, UK |
| Yunhe Gao | Rutgers University, USA |
| Zhe Xu | Chinese University of Hong Kong, China |
| Ziyang Wang | University of Oxford, UK |

## Acknowledgments

| | |
|---|---|
| Stephen Aylward | NVIDIA Corporation, USA |
| Daguang Xu | NVIDIA Corporation, USA |

# Contents

**Design and Assessment for Joint Systems and Workflows**

Beyond Manual Annotation: A Human-AI Collaborative Framework for Medical Image Segmentation Using Only "Better or Worse" Expert Feedback .................................................... 3
  *Yizhe Zhang*

A Methodology for Clinically Driven Interactive Segmentation Evaluation ..... 13
  *Parhom Esmaeili, Pedro Borges, Virginia Fernandez, Eli Gibson, Sebastien Ourselin, and M. Jorge Cardoso*

**Interactive Environments for Clinical Training, Education, and Human-AI Teaming**

Explainable AI for Automated User-Specific Feedback in Surgical Skill Acquisition ...................................................... 25
  *Catalina Gomez, Lalithkumar Seenivasan, Xinrui Zou, Jeewoo Yoon, Sirui Chu, Ariel Leong, Patrick Kramer, Yu-Chun Ku, Jose L. Porras, Alejandro Martin-Gomez, Masaru Ishii, and Mathias Unberath*

Real-Time, Dynamic, and Highly Generalizable Ultrasound Image Simulation-Guided Procedure Training System for Musculoskeletal Minimally Invasive Treatment ......................................... 35
  *Xiandi Wang, Zekun Jiang, Mengqi Tang, Ying Han, Dan Pu, and Kang Li*

**Human-in-the-Loop Model Training**

Learning What is Worth Learning: Active and Sequential Domain Adaptation for Multi-modal Gross Tumor Volume Segmentation ............. 47
  *Jingyun Yang, Guoqing Zhang, Jingge Wang, and Yang Li*

Guided Active Learning for Medical Image Segmentation .................. 58
  *Bernhard Föllmer, Vladimir Serafimoski, Kenrick Schulze, Federico Biavati, Sebastian Stober, Wojciech Samek, and Marc Dewey*

## Applications of Human-AI Interaction, Collaboration, and Human Factor Analysis

User Perception of Attention Visualizations: Effects on Interpretability Across Evidence-Based Medical Documents ............................. 71
   *Andrés Carvallo, Denis Parra, Peter Brusilovsky, Hernan Valdivieso, Gabriel Rada, Ivania Donoso, and Vladimir Araujo*

Simulating Inter-Observer Variability Across Clinical Experience Levels for Brain Tumour Segmentation ......................................... 81
   *Haley Gillett, Emma A. M. Stanley, Raissa Souza, Matthias Wilms, and Nils D. Forkert*

## Boosting Transparency, Interpretability, and Risk Management

Perceptual Evaluation of GANs and Diffusion Models for Generating X-Rays ......................................................... 93
   *Gregory Schuit, Denis Parra, and Cecilia Besa*

**Author Index** ....................................................... 103

# Design and Assessment for Joint Systems and Workflows

# Beyond Manual Annotation: A Human-AI Collaborative Framework for Medical Image Segmentation Using Only "Better or Worse" Expert Feedback

Yizhe Zhang(✉)

Nanjing University of Science and Technology, Nanjing, China
zhangyizhe@njust.edu.cn

**Abstract.** Manual annotation of medical images is a labor-intensive and time-consuming process, posing a significant bottleneck in the development and deployment of robust medical imaging AI systems. This paper introduces a novel hands-free Human-AI collaborative framework for medical image segmentation that substantially reduces the annotation burden by eliminating the need for explicit manual labeling. The core innovation lies in a preference learning paradigm, where human experts provide minimal, intuitive feedback—simply indicating whether an AI-generated segmentation is better or worse than a previous version. The framework comprises four key components: (1) an adaptable foundation model (FM) for feature extraction, (2) label propagation based on feature similarity, (3) a clicking agent that learns from human better-or-worse feedback to decide where to click and with which label, and (4) a multi-round segmentation learning procedure that trains a state-of-the-art segmentation network using pseudo-labels generated by the clicking agent and FM-based label propagation. Experiments on three public datasets demonstrate that the proposed approach achieves competitive segmentation performance using only binary preference feedback—without requiring experts to directly manually annotate the images.

**Keywords:** Human-AI Collaboration · Medical Image Segmentation · Preference Learning · Pseudo-labeling · Foundation Models

## 1 Introduction

The delineation of anatomical structures and pathological regions through image segmentation is a cornerstone of modern medical image analysis, critical for clinical diagnostics, treatment planning, and longitudinal studies [11,14]. The advent of deep learning, particularly convolutional neural networks (e.g., [8,16]) and transformer-based architectures (e.g., [6]), has led to state-of-the-art performance in numerous medical segmentation tasks. However, the success of these supervised learning models is predicated on the availability of large-scale, high-quality, pixel-level annotations. The generation of these annotations is a significant bottleneck, being notoriously slow, expensive, and requiring extensive

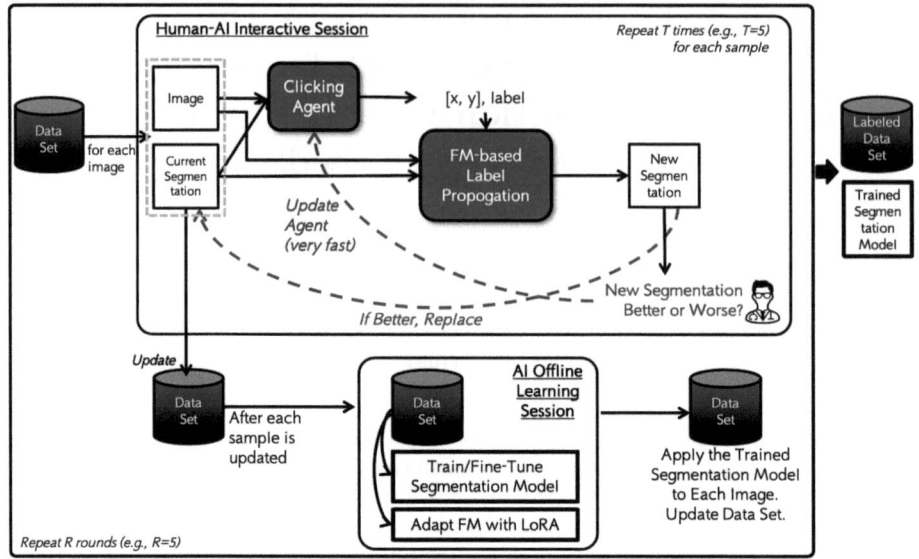

**Fig. 1.** Overview of the proposed framework.

domain expertise [5,13]. This reliance on meticulous manual labeling hinders the scalability and rapid deployment of AI-powered segmentation tools in diverse clinical settings.

To mitigate this annotation burden, the community has explored various weakly supervised and interactive segmentation paradigms. These methods aim to reduce the annotation effort by leveraging simpler forms of human guidance, such as bounding boxes, scribbles, or points [3,18]. More recently, the emergence of large-scale, pre-trained foundation models, such as the Segment Anything Model (SAM), has marked a significant shift [10]. These models, trained on vast datasets of natural images, exhibit remarkable zero-shot and few-shot generalization capabilities, enabling them to segment objects based on minimal user prompts like clicks or boxes. Adaptations of these models for the medical domain, such as MedSAM [15] and SAM-Med2D [4], have further demonstrated their potential to reduce annotation time.

Despite these advancements, existing interactive approaches, including those based on foundation models, still require the user to **manually** provide explicit and spatially precise inputs. The expert must still identify correct and incorrect regions, a task that, while simpler than full manual segmentation, can still be cognitively demanding and time-consuming, especially for complex 3D anatomies or subtle pathologies, especially for complex 3D anatomies or subtle pathologies [12]. Furthermore, these methods often necessitate multiple rounds of corrective interactions to refine the segmentation to a clinically acceptable standard.

A more intuitive and less burdensome form of expert feedback would be comparative. Often, a clinician can readily judge whether one segmentation output is "better" or "worse" than another, even if they cannot, or do not have the time to, pinpoint the exact locations of all errors. This type of preference-based feedback is natural to human decision-making and has the potential to significantly streamline the human-AI interaction process. Recent work has begun to explore the use of preference learning for model optimization, for instance, by using direct preference optimization to refine foundation models with simulated annotator rankings [11].

In this paper, we introduce a novel human-AI collaborative framework that moves beyond traditional explicit annotation and harnesses the power of simple, binary preference feedback. Our method entirely bypasses the need for manually providing pixel-level ground truth, instead learning to produce accurate segmentations from an expert's comparative judgments and feedback. The core of our framework is a learning-based clicking agent that, guided by "better or worse" signals from a human expert, intelligently samples points to generate pseudo-labels. These pseudo-labels, propagated in the rich feature space of a foundation model, are then used to train a pre-trained, state-of-the-art segmentation network. Our main contributions are:

- A novel human-AI collaborative segmentation framework that learns from minimal, non-local, binary preference feedback (i.e., "better or worse"), eliminating the need for any manual pixel-level and/or region-level annotation.
- A learning-based clicking agent that interprets the expert's preference feedback to strategically decide where to sample points and with which labels to generate high-quality pseudo-annotations.
- The integration of a foundation model for robust feature extraction and label propagation, enabling the generation of dense pseudo-labels from the sparse points provided by the clicking agent.
- A demonstration on multiple public medical imaging datasets that our preference-based approach can achieve competitive segmentation performance.

Our work represents a significant step toward more efficient, scalable, and user-friendly AI systems for medical image segmentation, enabling high-quality results even when detailed manual annotations are costly or impractical to obtain. A high-level overview of the proposed method is illustrated in Fig. 1.

## 2 Method

Our proposed Human-AI collaborative framework learns to segment medical images from simple "better or worse" feedback, obviating the need for manual pixel-level annotations. The framework operates in an iterative, multi-round process, where each round consists of two main stages: (1) an interactive pseudo-labeling stage where a clicking agent, guided by expert preference, generates sparse annotations that are propagated into dense pseudo-masks; and (2) a segmentation model training stage where a state-of-the-art network is trained on these pseudo-labels.

## 2.1 Adaptable Foundation Model for Feature Extraction

The cornerstone of our label propagation mechanism is a large, pre-trained foundation model. We employ DINOv2 [10] with a Vision Transformer (ViT) backbone, which provides a rich, patch-level feature space that captures fine-grained semantic and spatial relationships within the image. Given an input image, the model outputs a sequence of normalized feature vectors $\{f_i\}_{i=1}^{N}$, where $N$ is the number of patches.

To tailor the generic features of DINOv2 to the specific medical domain of the target dataset, we make the model adaptable. We employ Low-Rank Adaptation (LoRA) [7], which introduces trainable, low-rank matrices into the query and value projections of the transformer's self-attention layers. This allows us to efficiently fine-tune the feature extractor using a contrastive triplet loss on the pseudo-labeled data gathered during the interactive phase. This adaptation sharpens the feature space, improving the model's ability to distinguish between foreground and background tissue based on the evolving pseudo-annotations.

## 2.2 Clicking Agent and Label Propagation

**Preference-Based Clicking Agent.** We formalize the task of identifying informative correction locations as a Reinforcement Learning (RL) problem. We design a lightweight "clicking agent" whose goal is to learn an optimal policy for selecting click coordinates.

- State. The state $s_t$ at step $t$ is a multi-channel tensor representing the agent's current knowledge. It comprises the resized input image concatenated with the current generated segmentation mask. This provides the agent with both the original image context and the current state of the segmentation it needs to improve.
- Action. The agent's action $a_t$ is the selection of a single pixel coordinate $(y, x)$ on which to place a corrective click. The agent's policy is modeled by a small U-Net, which outputs a logit map over the input image space. An action is sampled from the resulting softmax probability distribution, with a temperature parameter to control exploration.
- Reward. The reward signal $r_t$ directly models the "better or worse" feedback. After the agent selects a click location, we use it to update the segmentation via label propagation. The resulting new segmentation mask is compared to the mask before the click. The reward is binary: $+1$ if expert consider the result gets better and $-1$ if it does not (a "worse" outcome). The agent's policy is updated using the REINFORCE algorithm [20], a policy gradient method that adjusts its parameters to favor actions that yield higher rewards and improve segmentation.

**DINO-Based Label Propagation.** A single click provides only sparse information. To generate a dense pseudo-mask for training the segmentation model, we propagate the click's label based on feature similarity. When a click is placed

**Algorithm 1.** Human-AI Collaborative Annotation using Preference Feedback
───────────────────────────────────────────────────────────────
1: **Initialize:** Segmentation model $S_{seg}$, Clicking Agent $A_{click}$, Adaptable Foundation Model $\mathcal{F}_{adapt}$ (DINOv2+LoRA).
2: **Input:** Dataset $\mathcal{D}$, number of rounds $R = 5$, interaction steps per image $T = 5$, similarity threshold $\tau = 0.8$.
3: **for** round $r = 1$ to $R$ **do**
4:     $\mathcal{P}_r \leftarrow \emptyset$     ▷ Initialize set of pseudo-labels for the current round
5:     **for** each image $I \in \mathcal{D}$ **do**
6:         Extract patch features $\{f_i\} \leftarrow \mathcal{F}_{adapt}(I)$
7:         $M_{current} \leftarrow S_{seg}(I)$   ▷ Get initial segmentation from the main segmentation model
8:         **for** step $t = 1$ to $T$ **do**
9:             Define state $s_t \leftarrow \text{concat}(I, M_{current})$
10:            Sample click action $a_t \sim A_{click}(s_t)$   ▷ Agent selects a click location
11:            $M_{new} \leftarrow \text{PropagateLabel}(a_t, \{f_i\}, \tau)$ ▷ Generate mask via DINO-based propagation
12:            $r_t \leftarrow \text{GetExpertPreference}(M_{new}, M_{current})$ ▷ Reward is +1 if better, −1 if worse
13:            Update $A_{click}$'s policy using $(s_t, a_t, r_t)$ via REINFORCE algorithm.
14:            **if** $r_t = +1$ **then**
15:                $M_{current} \leftarrow M_{new}$   ▷ Update mask only on improvement
16:            **end if**
17:         **end for**
18:         Add final pseudo-mask $M_{current}$ to $\mathcal{P}_r$.
19:     **end for**
20:     $\mathcal{P}_r \leftarrow \text{FilterTopK}(\mathcal{P}_r)$   ▷ Optional: Select highest-quality pseudo-labels
21:     Fine-tune $S_{seg}$ on $\mathcal{P}_r$.
22:     Adapt $\mathcal{F}_{adapt}$ on $\mathcal{P}_r$ using a contrastive triplet loss.
23: **end for**
24: **Return:** Fully trained segmentation model $S_{seg}$.
───────────────────────────────────────────────────────────────

at coordinate $(y, x)$ with label $l \in \{\text{foreground}, \text{background}\}$, we identify the corresponding feature vector $f_{click}$ from our adapted DINOv2 model. We then compute the cosine similarity between $f_{click}$ and all other patch features $\{f_i\}$ in the image. All patches whose feature similarity to $f_{click}$ exceeds a predefined threshold (e.g., 0.8) are assigned the label $l$. This process converts a few sparse clicks into a dense pseudo-label map.

### 2.3 Multi-round Segmentation Model Training

The pseudo-labels generated from the interactive process across the dataset form the training set for a dedicated segmentation network. At the end of each round, a segmentation model is trained or fine-tuned on the collection of newly generated pseudo-masks. The refined model from the current round then serves as the baseline model for the next round, providing progressively better initial segmentations for the agent to improve upon. This iterative refinement allows the model to learn complex anatomical features from simple preference feedback, bootstrapping its performance over several rounds. To further enhance performance, we optionally filter the generated pseudo-labels, using only the top-K percent high quality pseudo-labels to train the segmentation model. The complete procedure of the proposed method is outlined in Algorithm 1.

## 3 Experiments

We conducted a series of experiments to validate our proposed framework's ability to generate high-quality pseudo-labels and train an effective segmentation model using only preference-based feedback ("better or worse" feedback). Our evaluation is performed on three distinct and publicly available medical image segmentation datasets, covering different modalities and anatomical targets.

**Breast Ultrasound Segmentation.** To evaluate our method on ultrasound imagery, we use the Breast Ultrasound Images (BUSI) dataset [1]. This dataset contains 780 ultrasound scans categorized as normal, benign, and malignant, each with a corresponding ground truth mask. As the original release does not specify a train/test split, we utilize the complete dataset for our experiments.

**Skin Lesion Segmentation.** For dermoscopic image analysis, we use the training set from the ISIC 2018 Challenge [17]. This set contains 2594 images of skin lesions with corresponding binary segmentation masks. Similar to the polyp dataset, we use all provided training images to validate the proposed method.

**Polyp Segmentation.** We use 1,450 colonoscopy images collected from two polyp segmentation datasets: Kvasir-SEG [9] and CVC-ClinicDB [2]. All images are accompanied by high-quality manual segmentation masks. The combined dataset captures a wide range of polyp sizes, shapes, and appearances.

### 3.1 Experimental Setup

We use the provided ground truth masks in these datasets only as an **oracle** to simulate the expert's "better or worse" feedback, not as supervised training masks for the segmentation model. We compute the Dice Similarity Coefficient (DSC) between the oracle and the segmentation mask both before and after the agent's click. If the DSC increases, the outcome is labeled "better" (reward = +1). If not, it is labeled "worse" (reward = −1). This binary signal is the sole feedback used to train the clicking agent. We set the number of learning rounds to 5 across all experiments. In each round, every image receives 5 clicks from the clicking agent. A PVT-based [19] segmentation model, i.e., HSNet [21], is employed as the main segmentation network for all experiments. To assess the quality of the final annotations produced by the framework, the segmentation model was evaluated on the same data used for the interactive, feedback-based training. A next step, which we leave for future work, is to use the generated dataset to train a model and evaluate its generalization performance on unseen data.

### 3.2 Results and Analyses

In Fig. 2, we present the end-of-round segmentation performance across three diverse medical image segmentation tasks: polyp segmentation, skin lesion segmentation, and ultrasound image segmentation. As the annotation rounds progress, we observe a consistent improvement in segmentation quality across all datasets, evidenced by increasing Dice scores and decreasing Hausdorff Distance at 95th percentile (HD95). This trend demonstrates the effectiveness of our

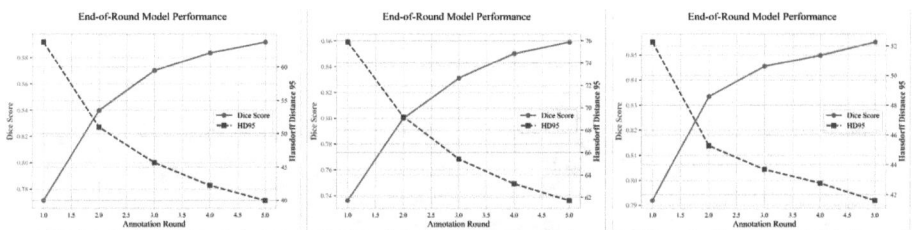

**Fig. 2.** Segmentation performance across annotation rounds, showing progressive improvement with increasing Dice scores and decreasing HD95 on polyp (left), skin lesion (middle), and ultrasound (right) datasets.

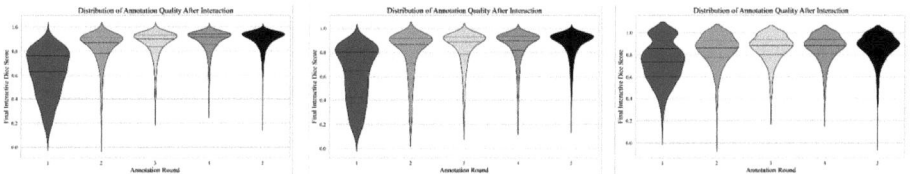

**Fig. 3.** Violin plots showing the distribution of final interactive Dice scores across annotation rounds, highlighting improved annotation quality and consistency over time. Results are shown for polyp (left), skin lesion (middle), and ultrasound (right) datasets.

proposed human-AI collaborative framework in incrementally enhancing model performance through minimal expert feedback.

Figure 3 illustrates the distribution of segmentation quality, measured by the Dice score, after each round of interaction across the three datasets: polyp, skin lesion, ultrasound. Across all tasks, we observe a clear shift in the distribution toward higher Dice scores as annotation rounds progress, indicating that both the average and consistency of segmentation quality improve with our method. Notably, the initial annotation round exhibits a wide and often bimodal distribution, reflecting substantial variability in interaction effectiveness. However, from the second round onward, the distributions become increasingly concentrated around higher Dice scores (often exceeding 0.8), demonstrating that our clicking agent, guided by simple "better or worse" feedback, learns to produce more accurate and reliable annotations over time. Figure 4, Fig. 5, and Fig. 6 present visualizations of the segmentation results. Although our method performs well overall, certain cases still highlight areas for potential improvement.

## 4 Limitations

Despite promising results, our framework has limitations. First, we rely on a simulated oracle that compares Dice scores to generate "better or worse" feedback. While this enables controlled evaluation, it oversimplifies real-world expert judgments, which are often subjective and prioritize clinical relevance over global

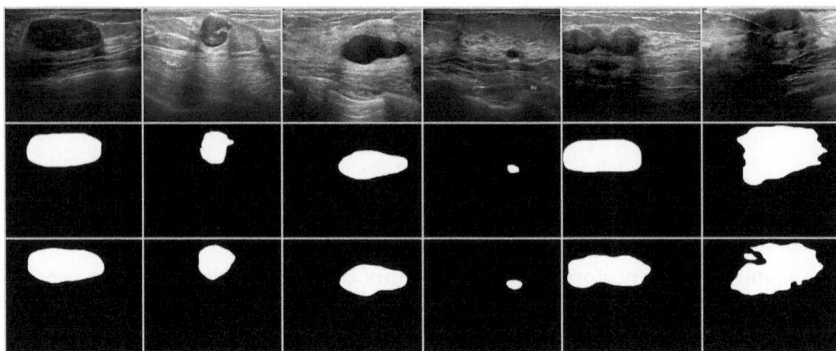

**Fig. 4.** Segmentation examples on the BUSI dataset. Top: input ultrasound image; Middle: ground truth; Bottom: segmentation by our method.

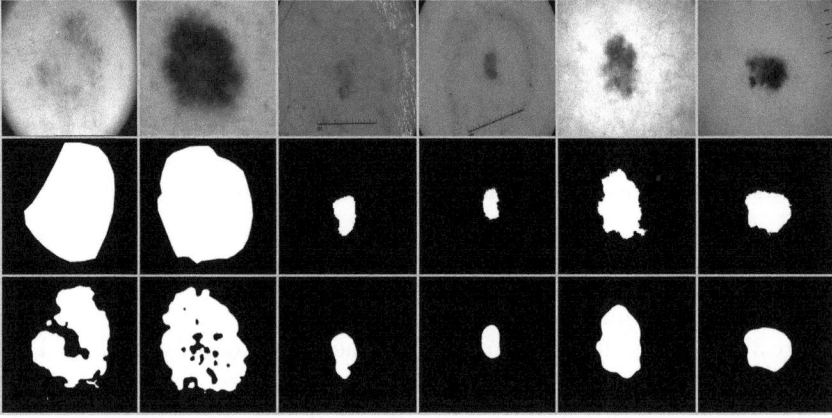

**Fig. 5.** Segmentation examples on the skin lesion dataset. Top: input dermoscopy image; Middle: ground truth mask; Bottom: segmentation generated by our method.

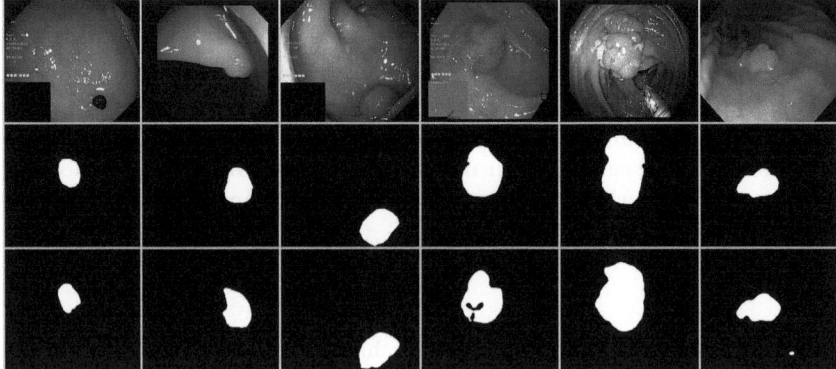

**Fig. 6.** Segmentation examples on the polyp dataset. Top: input endoscopic image; Middle: ground truth mask; Bottom: segmentation generated by our method.

metrics. Human feedback also introduces variability and cognitive bias not captured by our oracle. Second, the learning efficiency of the clicking agent remains a challenge. The REINFORCE-based training suffers from high variance and sparse binary rewards, which may delay convergence and require many interactions before the agent becomes effective.

## 5 Conclusion

This paper tackles the persistent bottleneck of manual annotation in medical image segmentation by introducing a novel human-AI collaborative framework that learns entirely from "better or worse" expert feedback. We have demonstrated that by combining a learning-based clicking agent, a pre-trained foundation model for feature extraction and label propagation, and a multi-round training strategy, it is possible to train a high-performance segmentation network without requiring any direct manual annotation from users. Our experiments across polyp, skin lesion, and breast ultrasound datasets validate that this minimal form of feedback is sufficient to achieve competitive segmentation accuracy. This work marks a promising step towards creating more intuitive, efficient, and scalable AI systems for medical imaging, potentially shifting the human's role from a tedious annotator to a high-level critic.

**Acknowledgments.** This research was supported in part by the Natural Science Foundation of Jiangsu Province (Grant BK20220949), and National Natural Science Foundation of China (Grant 62201263).

**Disclosure of Interests.** The authors have no competing interests to declare that are relevant to the content of this article.

## References

1. Al-Dhabyani, W., Gomaa, M., Khaled, H., Fahmy, A.: Dataset of breast ultrasound images. Data Brief **28**, 104863 (2020)
2. Bernal, J., Sánchez, F.J., Fernández-Esparrach, G., Gil, D., Rodríguez, C., Vilariño, F.: WM-DOVA maps for accurate polyp highlighting in colonoscopy: Validation vs. saliency maps from physicians. Comput. Med. Imaging Graph. **43**, 99–111 (2015)
3. Can, Y.B., Chaitanya, K., Mustafa, B., Koch, L.M., Konukoglu, E., Baumgartner, C.F.: Learning to segment medical images with scribble-supervision alone. In: Stoyanov, D., et al. (eds.) DLMIA/ML-CDS -2018. LNCS, vol. 11045, pp. 236–244. Springer, Cham (2018). https://doi.org/10.1007/978-3-030-00889-5_27
4. Cheng, J., et al.: SAM-MED2D. arXiv preprint arXiv:2308.16184 (2023)
5. Cheplygina, V., de Bruijne, M., Pluim, J.P.: Not-so-supervised: a survey of semi-supervised, multi-instance, and transfer learning in medical image analysis. Med. Image Anal. **54**, 280–296 (2019)
6. Dosovitskiy, A., et al.: An image is worth 16x16 words: transformers for image recognition at scale. In: International Conference on Learning Representations (2021)

7. Hu, E.J., et al.: LORA: low-rank adaptation of large language models. ICLR **1**(2), 3 (2022)
8. Isensee, F., Jaeger, P.F., Kohl, S.A., Petersen, J., Maier-Hein, K.H.: NNU-Net: a self-configuring method for deep learning-based biomedical image segmentation. Nat. Methods **18**(2), 203–211 (2021)
9. Jha, D., et al.: KVASIR-SEG: a segmented polyp dataset. In: Ro, Y.M., et al. (eds.) MMM 2020. LNCS, vol. 11962, pp. 451–462. Springer, Cham (2020). https://doi.org/10.1007/978-3-030-37734-2_37
10. Kirillov, A., et al.: Segment anything. In: Proceedings of the IEEE/CVF International Conference on Computer Vision, pp. 3879–3893 (2023)
11. Konwer, A., et al.: Enhancing SAM with efficient prompting and preference optimization for semi-supervised medical image segmentation. In: Proceedings of the Computer Vision and Pattern Recognition Conference, pp. 20990–21000 (2025)
12. Liao, X., et al.: Iteratively-refined interactive 3D medical image segmentation with multi-agent reinforcement learning. In: Proceedings of the IEEE/CVF Conference on Computer Vision and Pattern Recognition, pp. 9394–9402 (2020)
13. Liao, Z., Hu, S., Xie, Y., Xia, Y.: Modeling annotator preference and stochastic annotation error for medical image segmentation. Med. Image Anal. **92**, 103028 (2024)
14. Litjens, G., et al.: A survey on deep learning in medical image analysis. Med. Image Anal. **42**, 60–88 (2017)
15. Ma, J., He, Y., Li, F., Han, L., You, C., Wang, B.: Segment anything in medical images. Nat. Commun. **15**(1), 654 (2024)
16. Ronneberger, O., Fischer, P., Brox, T.: U-Net: convolutional networks for biomedical image segmentation. In: Navab, N., Hornegger, J., Wells, W.M., Frangi, A.F. (eds.) MICCAI 2015. LNCS, vol. 9351, pp. 234–241. Springer, Cham (2015). https://doi.org/10.1007/978-3-319-24574-4_28
17. Tschandl, P., Rosendahl, C., Kittler, H.: The ham10000 dataset, a large collection of multi-source dermatoscopic images of common pigmented skin lesions. Sci. Data **5**(1), 1–9 (2018)
18. Wang, G., et al.: Interactive medical image segmentation using deep learning with image-specific fine tuning. IEEE Trans. Med. Imaging **37**(7), 1562–1573 (2018)
19. Wang, W., et al.: PVT V2: improved baselines with pyramid vision transformer. Comput. Vis. Media **8**(3), 415–424 (2022)
20. Williams, R.J.: Simple statistical gradient-following algorithms for connectionist reinforcement learning. Mach. Learn. **8**, 229–256 (1992)
21. Zhang, W., Fu, C., Zheng, Y., Zhang, F., Zhao, Y., Sham, C.W.: HSNet: a hybrid semantic network for polyp segmentation. Comput. Biol. Med. **150**, 106173 (2022)

# A Methodology for Clinically Driven Interactive Segmentation Evaluation

Parhom Esmaeili[1](✉), Pedro Borges[1], Virginia Fernandez[1], Eli Gibson[2], Sebastien Ourselin[1], and M. Jorge Cardoso[1]

[1] School of Biomedical Engineering and Imaging Sciences, KCL, London, UK
parhom.esmaeili@kcl.ac.uk
[2] Siemens Healthineers, Princeton, NJ, USA

**Abstract.** Interactive segmentation is a promising strategy for building robust, generalisable algorithms for volumetric medical image segmentation. However, inconsistent and clinically unrealistic evaluation hinders fair comparison and misrepresents real-world performance. We propose a clinically grounded methodology for defining evaluation tasks and metrics, and built a software framework for constructing standardised evaluation pipelines. We evaluate state-of-the-art algorithms across heterogeneous and complex tasks and observe that **(i)** minimising information loss when processing user interactions is critical for model robustness, **(ii)** adaptive-zooming mechanisms boost robustness and speed convergence, **(iii)** performance drops if validation prompting behaviour/budgets differ from training, **(iv)** 2D methods perform well with slab-like images and coarse targets, but 3D context helps with large or irregularly shaped targets, **(v)** performance of non-medical-domain models (e.g. SAM2) degrades with poor contrast and complex shapes.

**Keywords:** Validation · Interactive Segmentation · Data Annotation

## 1 Introduction

Segmentation of anatomical structures and pathologies is essential for extracting imaging biomarkers and delineating structures for use in treatment planning, patient monitoring, and guided therapies. However, manual segmentation of imaging volumes remains time-consuming and bottlenecks clinical workflows [13]. While automatic segmentation algorithms trained via supervised learning have demonstrated strong performance on many targets [8], fine structures, heterogeneous and out-of-distribution targets/modalities can be particularly hard. Moreover, the limited availability of annotated data, caused by data sharing restrictions [12] and laboriousness of manual annotation often hinders automated segmentation performance. Algorithms with strong zero-shot generalisation and semi-automated refinement, especially if they can improve on tasks with repeated exposure and reach expert-level performance, would provide substantial clinical impact. Interactive segmentation incorporates user prompts to

© The Author(s), under exclusive license to Springer Nature Switzerland AG 2026
X. Guo et al. (Eds.): HAIC 2025, LNCS 16214, pp. 13–22, 2026.
https://doi.org/10.1007/978-3-032-08970-0_2

guide and refine segmentations, helping to address many of these challenges by reducing reliance on image-derived features. Classical interactive methods relying on low-level image features [3,10] are already integrated into segmentation tools such as ITK-Snap and 3D Slicer [6,20] but often struggle with low-contrast or complex tissue boundaries. Recently, deep learning-based interactive segmentation has advanced in natural [11,17] and medical imaging domains [4,5,9,14,19]. However, current approaches to validate and compare interactive segmentation algorithms are flawed, preventing fair assessment and overestimating progress. This paper outlines key pitfalls, offers guidelines, proposes a framework for constructing evaluation pipelines, and analyses prominent algorithms using these.

## 2 Validation Pitfalls

In a clinical setting, interactive segmentation algorithms are AI-assistants that translate user inputs and prompts into model-ready formats and return segmentations in the original image space. However, most algorithmic validation experiments fail to appropriately standardise the representation of the inputs, prompts and outputs by introducing pre-processing steps such as: **(i)** resampling to model-specific resolutions for prompting and validation [5,19]; or **(ii)** simulating prompts and calculating metrics on restrictive image subregions (e.g., slices or annotation-informed image crops) [4,14,19]. Since the number of interactions and inference times are often used as a efficiency proxy, reporting metrics on a sub-region [14] misrepresents annotation-effort and hampers comparison. Performing evaluation in the original image space (full resolution and field-of-view) is recommended to better reflect deployment realities.

### 2.1 Task Taxonomies

Here we outline a task taxonomy covering algorithmic axes of complexity; essential for clinicians to select interactive segmentation algorithms suited to their applications, and to aid researchers in identifying remaining challenges. We also suggest suitable evaluation principles, where applicable.

**Problem 1:** Ulrich et al. [18] note that most studies focus on segmentation tasks easily handled by automated methods, neglecting clinically difficult cases. Challenging tasks include targets with ambiguous boundaries or heterogeneous appearance (e.g., tumours), very small targets (white matter lesions), geometrically complex or topologically constrained structures (like vascular networks), and multi-target segmentation where simple label merging is suboptimal (e.g., nested or adjacent semantic targets, or when spatial contiguity does not define separate instances). Interactive segmentation is also often evaluated as binary instance segmentation, even in multi-target cases, with benchmarks [18] relying on potentially unreliable assumptions of contiguity for identifying instances (e.g., touching lesions may be distinct metastases). Evaluations should prioritise challenging tasks, assess multi-target segmentation in parallel for tasks where simple labels merging is inadequate, and critically assess contiguity-based assumptions.

**Problem 2:** Most studies omit multi-modal (e.g., PET-CT [7]) or multi-sequence (e.g., mpMRI [16]) image data even when it provides essential clinical context. Validation pipelines should aim to include these, when applicable to the task, to foster development of more clinically impactful algorithms.

**Problem 3:** Zero-shot models are mainly trained and tested in case independent and fully interactive settings. Evaluation tasks testing automatic initialisation techniques or model adaptation to repeated tasks (e.g. fine tuning, active learning) could foster algorithms which further expedite annotation.

**Problem 4:** Prompting methods (points, scribbles, boxes, lassos) differ in effectiveness and annotation effort due to variation in implied intent and spatial constraints (e.g., lassos are laborious for jagged shapes). Also, some algorithms fully support all prompts during initialisation and editing [9], while others only support a subset of prompts in specific circumstances [4,5,17]. For a fair evaluation one should consider using prompt configurations that are supported by all the algorithms being compared. User-effort should also be estimated using the number of interactions and also ideally the prompt placement effort as proxies, with placement efforts being estimated via user studies. This approach could also facilitate effort comparisons across prompting mechanisms.

### 2.2 Metrics

As recommended by Maier-Hein et al. [15], evaluations should report complementary metrics that measure different aspects of the task, e.g. both overlap based metrics (e.g., Dice) and boundary-aware metrics (e.g., normalised surface Dice, NSD). Yet, many studies and even benchmarks [18] rely solely on Dice, which can misrepresent performance on small and fine, or geometrically complex structures. Performance variability during iterative refinement is also rarely captured, despite its importance; Dice and NSD area under the curve (AUC) metrics normalised by interaction count [2] can be used to measure convergence speed and stability. As AUC may penalise methods that require more interactions but that yield a better final outcome, especially under tight interaction budgets, assessing convergence to clinically meaningful endpoints is important. Existing benchmarks also only assume zero-shot settings for clinical use overlooking comparisons to strong automated methods [18], such as nnU-Net [8], which can offer lower annotator effort on repeated tasks. Evaluations should consider larger interaction budgets to identify emergent behaviours and use clinical criteria or task-specialist automatic baselines to determine termination criteria. The latter can also highlight any superiority of interactive methods in clinical workflows.

## 3 Methods

The interactive nature of these algorithms requires continuous communication between the algorithm and a validation framework. Therefore, we developed a modular framework that decouples the generation of segmentation requests (image patch, prompts, task description) and metric computation from the inference algorithm; and integrated this into a task selection pipeline (Fig. 1). First, we characterise algorithms with characteristics, or fingerprints, spanning:**(i)** whether algorithms are static at inference or learn to adapt over repeated tasks; **(ii)** supported inference modes (initialisation strategies and whether editing is natively supported or partially compatible); **(iii)** segmentation subtypes supported natively (e.g., binary, multi-class, semantic, instance, or panoptic segmentation); **(iv)** general-purpose versus target-specific training; **(v)** compatibility across prompt types (points, scribbles, bounding boxes, lassos), and any constraints on their usage (see Sect. 2.1); **(vi)** model-native image patch configurations (voxel counts, channel count) and algorithmic adaptability to deviations from these; and **(vii)** the imaging modalities seen during training. These fingerprints need to be cross-referenced with candidate tasks, defined by: dataset, segmentation subtype and target, image patch configuration (voxel count, channel count, modality and sequence) and prompt specification to select compatible tasks. The task then determines the corresponding evaluation metrics, while the algorithm fingerprints define compatible prompting mechanisms.

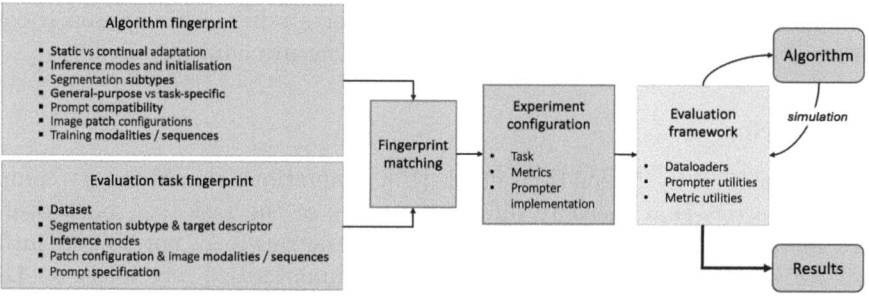

**Fig. 1.** A flowchart for identifying compatible experiments that are passed to the proposed evaluation framework for interaction simulation and evaluation.

We integrated SAM2 [17], SAM-Med2D [4], SAM-Med3D [19], and SegVol [5] into applications compatible with the proposed framework's segmentation request definition (image-patch, corresponding prompt coordinates and the segmentation task description). Model fingerprints are shown in Fig. 2, all applications were kept online throughout experimental sessions. For SAM2 and SAM-Med2D images intensities were clipped (0.5-99.5th percentiles) and min-max normalised to [0,255] on full volumes. Inference for 2D models is performed on axial slices with images and prompt coordinates remapped to native voxel counts. Outputs are then remapped to input voxel counts. No changes were needed for SAM-Med3D as it provided native normalisation and voxel count adaptation. SegVol lacked voxel count adaptation for points, so points were translated into relative coordinates for the cropped zoom-in region, and then remapped to native voxel counts for zoom-out inference. No algorithmic changes were made beyond those mentioned above.

| Algorithm | Static | Inference Modes | | Seg. Type | General Purpose | Interaction Prompts | | | | | Image Data Configs | | | | Modality |
|---|---|---|---|---|---|---|---|---|---|---|---|---|---|---|---|
| | | Edit | Auto | | | Point | Scribble | Bounding Box | Lasso | | Patch Config. | | | | |
| | | | | | | | | | | Spatial Voxel Count | Spatial Flexibility | Channel Count | Channel Flexibility | | |
| SAM2 | ✓ | ✓ Implicit | ✗ | Binary Semantic | ✓ | ✓ | ~ (Point Set) | | ✓ | ✗ | $1024^2$ | ~ | 3 (RGB) | ~ | RGB |
| SAM-Med2D | ✓ | ✓ Implicit | ✗ | Binary Semantic | ✓ | ✓ | ~ (Point Set) | | ✓ | ✗ | $256^2$ | ~ | 3 | ✗ | CT/MRI/Ultrasound/Microscopy/PET/RGB |
| SAM-Med3D | ✓ | ✓ Explicit | ✗ | Binary Semantic | ✓ | ✓ | ✗ | ✗ | ✗ | | $128^3$ | ~ | 1 | ✗ | CT/MRI |
| SegVol | ✓ | ~ (Atom) | ✗ | Binary Semantic | ✓ | ✓ | ~ (Point Set) | | ✓ | ✗ | 32 x 256 x 256 | ~ | 1 | ✗ | CT |

**Fig. 2.** Algorithm fingerprints. Ticks: full support; Tildes: partial support; Crosses: no support. Implicit editing uses full prompt memory, explicit only uses current prompts, and atomic editing re-does inference with full prompt memory. All except SAM-Med3D support scribbles (represented as a set of points); SAM-Med3D is limited by a one-point-per-class constraint. Only SAM2 natively supports multi-channel radiological images.

## 4 Experiments and Results

Given the fundamental pitfalls described in Sect. 2 we focus on the challenges vital to clinical deployment—conducting evaluations in the native image spaces. We pick four axes of algorithmic complexity: **(i)** voxel count (i.e. volume size), **(ii)** image spacing/anisotropy, **(iii)** target geometry (spherical vs irregular), and **(iv)** target size variation. We chose binary semantic segmentation tasks from the Medical Segmentation Decathlon (MSD) [1], restricted by algorithmic fingerprints (Fig. 2), both because they capture the axes of complexity described above and for reproducibility. For multi-sequence datasets, the sequence best visualising the target was used. Tasks include whole hippocampus (small volume), brain tumour core (T2w; medium volume, irregular shape, isotropic), whole pancreas (large volume and target), whole prostate (T2w; spherical target, highly anisotropic), and lung lesion (largest component; small target in large volume). All simulations use one point per iteration per class (as it is a SAM-Med3D constraint), uniform randomly sampled from false-negative foreground and background regions computed between predictions and reference annotations. Simulations are fully interactive with 100 editing steps; SegVol uses atomic inference (Sect. 3). Per-sample evaluation uses Dice and NSD (MSD tolerances) per iteration, and interaction count normalised AUCs (nAUC). These metrics are reported with dataset-wide medians. nnU-Net [8] models were also trained with 2-fold cross-validation (due to limited compute) with optimal configuration selection. We then used the segmentation performance of nnU-Net trained on the full dataset as a target performance level. We chose task-specific lower quartile Dice score rather than mean performance due to nnU-Net's asymmetric, heavy-tailed Dice distributions. With this target performance, we then estimate the number of interactions (NoI) for convergence on a per-sample Dice basis;

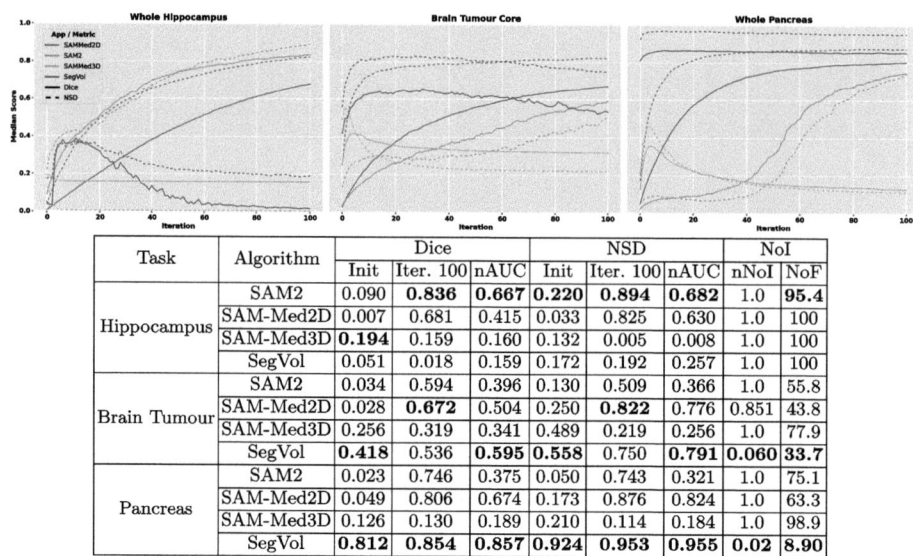

| Task | Algorithm | Dice | | | NSD | | | NoI | |
|---|---|---|---|---|---|---|---|---|---|
| | | Init | Iter. 100 | nAUC | Init | Iter. 100 | nAUC | nNoI | NoF |
| Hippocampus | SAM2 | 0.090 | **0.836** | **0.667** | 0.220 | **0.894** | **0.682** | 1.0 | **95.4** |
| | SAM-Med2D | 0.007 | 0.681 | 0.415 | 0.033 | 0.825 | 0.630 | 1.0 | 100 |
| | SAM-Med3D | **0.194** | 0.159 | 0.160 | 0.132 | 0.005 | 0.008 | 1.0 | 100 |
| | SegVol | 0.051 | 0.018 | 0.159 | 0.172 | 0.192 | 0.257 | 1.0 | 100 |
| Brain Tumour | SAM2 | 0.034 | 0.594 | 0.396 | 0.130 | 0.509 | 0.366 | 1.0 | 55.8 |
| | SAM-Med2D | 0.028 | **0.672** | 0.504 | 0.250 | **0.822** | 0.776 | 0.851 | 43.8 |
| | SAM-Med3D | 0.256 | 0.319 | 0.341 | 0.489 | 0.219 | 0.256 | 1.0 | 77.9 |
| | SegVol | **0.418** | 0.536 | **0.595** | **0.558** | 0.750 | **0.791** | **0.060** | **33.7** |
| Pancreas | SAM2 | 0.023 | 0.746 | 0.375 | 0.050 | 0.743 | 0.321 | 1.0 | 75.1 |
| | SAM-Med2D | 0.049 | 0.806 | 0.674 | 0.173 | 0.876 | 0.824 | 1.0 | 63.3 |
| | SAM-Med3D | 0.126 | 0.130 | 0.189 | 0.210 | 0.114 | 0.184 | 1.0 | 98.9 |
| | SegVol | **0.812** | **0.854** | **0.857** | **0.924** | **0.953** | **0.955** | **0.02** | **8.90** |

**Fig. 3. Top:** Median Dice and NSD across the refinement simulations as image voxel count increases (hippocampus, brain tumour core, pancreas). **Bottom:** Summary metrics for experiment 1; all metrics but NoF report dataset medians, NoF reports percentages. Bold indicates best metric per task.

the median NoI is then normalised by interaction count (nNoI). The fraction of samples that did not reach the performance target (NoF) is also reported.

**Experiment 1 - Image Voxel Count:** As shown in Fig. 3, 2D methods trail 3D ones in low-interaction settings across tasks. However, for small-volume hippocampus, both 2D models exceed the best 3D peak (SegVol) within 40 interactions. SAM2 achieves the highest final Dice, NSD, and nAUC scores, and is the only method to ever converge. For medium volumes (tumour core) we observed that 2D methods need more interactions to surpass the best 3D method (SegVol). SAM-Med2D obtains best peak and final Dice and NSD scores but SegVol performs better for the first 60 interactions with superior nAUC, nNoI, and NoF scores highlighting its rapid convergence. In large volumes (pancreas), SegVol performs best across iterations, maintaining strong leads in all metrics; converging rapidly and consistently with its zoom-out zoom-in mechanism (strongest nNoI and NoF scores). SAM-Med3D performs poorly due to lossy point mapping, retaining only foreground points and randomly sampling from point-centered resampled boxes for inference. Also, we note that SegVol improves initially but degrades with further interactions across tasks. This is pronounced in smaller volumes, suggesting densely packed points may induce undersegmentation.

**Experiment 2 - Image Anisotropy:** Figure 4 shows that 3D algorithms perform better at initialisation for both tasks. But, on slab-like images (prostate),

2D methods improve rapidly, becoming competitive after a few interactions. Around 30 iterations, 2D methods surpass the best 3D method (SegVol) in Dice and NSD, with fewer convergence failures (NoF). SAM2 achieves the best overall performance except in initialisation metrics, with no convergence failures. For isotropic images (tumour core), 2D methods are less competitive. SAM-Med2D achieves highest final and peak Dice and NSD but only surpasses SegVol after 60 edits which consistently converges rapidly across most metrics.

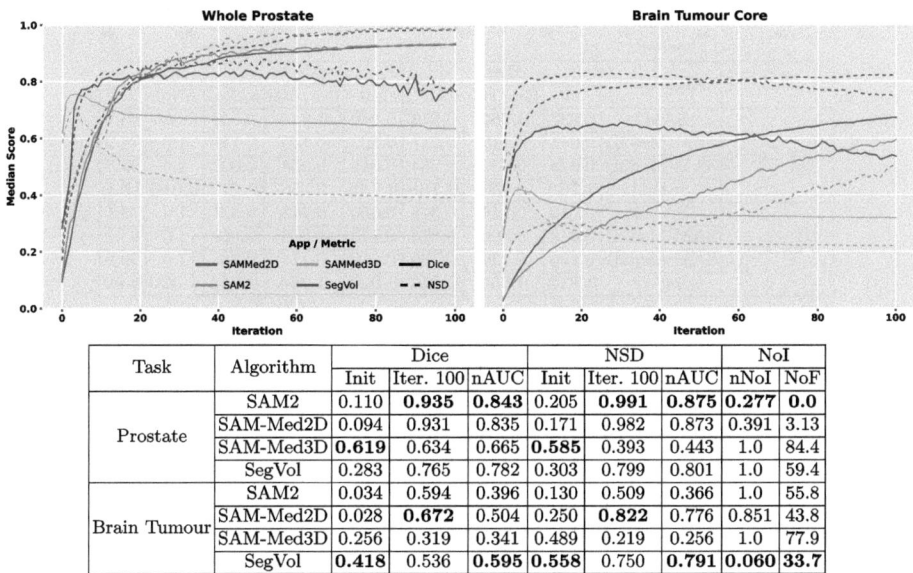

| Task | Algorithm | Dice | | | NSD | | | NoI | |
|---|---|---|---|---|---|---|---|---|---|
| | | Init | Iter. 100 | nAUC | Init | Iter. 100 | nAUC | nNoI | NoF |
| Prostate | SAM2 | 0.110 | **0.935** | **0.843** | 0.205 | **0.991** | **0.875** | **0.277** | **0.0** |
| | SAM-Med2D | 0.094 | 0.931 | 0.835 | 0.171 | 0.982 | 0.873 | 0.391 | 3.13 |
| | SAM-Med3D | **0.619** | 0.634 | 0.665 | **0.585** | 0.393 | 0.443 | 1.0 | 84.4 |
| | SegVol | 0.283 | 0.765 | 0.782 | 0.303 | 0.799 | 0.801 | 1.0 | 59.4 |
| Brain Tumour | SAM2 | 0.034 | 0.594 | 0.396 | 0.130 | 0.509 | 0.366 | 1.0 | 55.8 |
| | SAM-Med2D | 0.028 | **0.672** | 0.504 | 0.250 | **0.822** | 0.776 | 0.851 | 43.8 |
| | SAM-Med3D | 0.256 | 0.319 | 0.341 | 0.489 | 0.219 | 0.256 | 1.0 | 77.9 |
| | SegVol | **0.418** | 0.536 | **0.595** | **0.558** | 0.750 | **0.791** | **0.060** | **33.7** |

**Fig. 4. Top:** Median Dice and NSD across refinement simulations for the whole prostate and brain tumour core tasks. Axes of complexity: Highly anisotropic versus isotropic images, and spherical targets versus irregularly shaped targets. **Bottom:** Summary metrics for experiments 2 & 3; all metrics but NoF report dataset medians, NoF reports percentages. Bold indicates best metric per task.

**Experiment 3 - Target Geometry:** Figure 4 shows that SAM-Med3D has its best performance across any task for whole prostate. Considerable degradation on tumour core is due to SAM-Med3D's lossy prompt mapping preventing correction of oversegmentations; vital for non-coarse, non-spherical targets. SAM2 delivers best overall performance on whole prostate but performs worse than SAM-Med2D on tumour core, indicating medical-domain adaptation for irregular, ambiguous targets is important for points. SegVol's strong peak Dice and NSD metrics; and best nAUC, nNoI and NoF metrics on tumour core indicate volumetric context is key to rapid, consistent convergence on irregular structures.

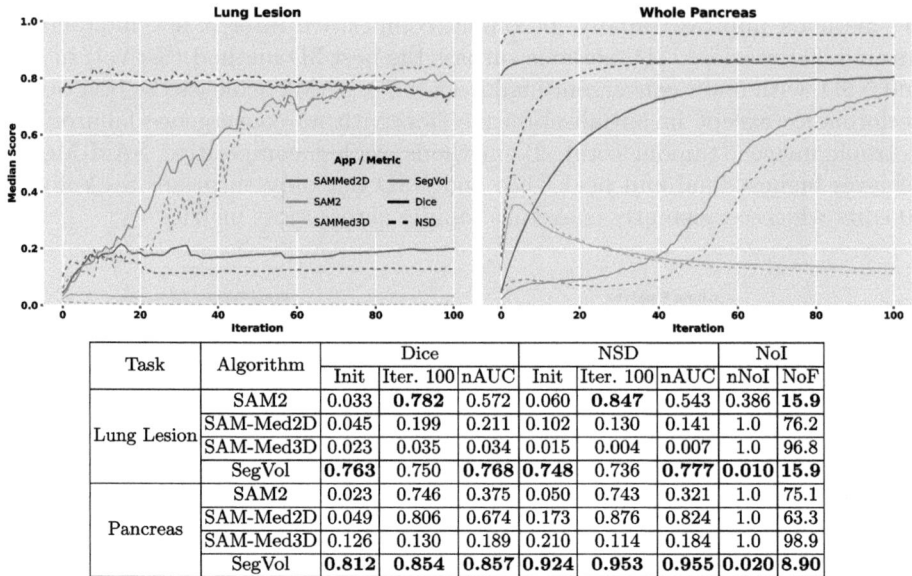

| Task | Algorithm | Dice | | | NSD | | | NoI | |
|---|---|---|---|---|---|---|---|---|---|
| | | Init | Iter. 100 | nAUC | Init | Iter. 100 | nAUC | nNoI | NoF |
| Lung Lesion | SAM2 | 0.033 | **0.782** | 0.572 | 0.060 | **0.847** | 0.543 | 0.386 | **15.9** |
| | SAM-Med2D | 0.045 | 0.199 | 0.211 | 0.102 | 0.130 | 0.141 | 1.0 | 76.2 |
| | SAM-Med3D | 0.023 | 0.035 | 0.034 | 0.015 | 0.004 | 0.007 | 1.0 | 96.8 |
| | SegVol | **0.763** | 0.750 | **0.768** | **0.748** | 0.736 | **0.777** | **0.010** | **15.9** |
| Pancreas | SAM2 | 0.023 | 0.746 | 0.375 | 0.050 | 0.743 | 0.321 | 1.0 | 75.1 |
| | SAM-Med2D | 0.049 | 0.806 | 0.674 | 0.173 | 0.876 | 0.824 | 1.0 | 63.3 |
| | SAM-Med3D | 0.126 | 0.130 | 0.189 | 0.210 | 0.114 | 0.184 | 1.0 | 98.9 |
| | SegVol | **0.812** | **0.854** | **0.857** | **0.924** | **0.953** | **0.955** | **0.020** | **8.90** |

**Fig. 5. Top:** Median Dice and NSD across refinement simulations for variation in target size relative to the image volume (lung lesion versus whole pancreas). Summary metrics for experiment 4; all metrics but NoF report dataset medians, NoF reports percentages. Bold indicates best metric per task.

**Experiment 4 - Target Size:** As shown in Fig. 5, for lung lesion (small target), SAM-Med2D performs poorly throughout. This is likely due to removing small targets from training data, improving in larger pancreas targets. SAM-Med3D struggles on both tasks, especially small targets, due to noisy point mapping to model-space. For lung lesion, although SAM2 reaches best peak Dice and NSD, SegVol converges faster with superior nAUC and nNoI and comparable failure rates. For the larger pancreas targets, SAM2 converges slower, while SegVol still achieves best performance across all metrics. The sizeable margin from the second best method on pancreas (SAM-Med2D) for Dice, NSD and NoF indicates volumetric context is vital for performance. Lastly, SegVol's robustness across target-size variation outlines the utility of dynamically adapting to target size.

## 5 Conclusions and Future Work

The proposed framework and evaluation highlights several takeaways: **(i)** minimising information loss when processing prompts and using adaptive zooming strategies enables robustness across variation in volume and target sizes **(ii)** adaptive zooming strategies enable rapid convergence **(iii)** performance can degrade if prompting behaviour or budgets diverge from that in training; **(iv)** 2D methods can excel on image-slabs with coarse targets, but volumetric context aids in large or irregularly shaped targets, even for out-of-distribution modalities (e.g., SegVol for tumour core); **(v)** SAM2 can perform well without medical-domain training but suffers on tissue-ambiguous targets like brain tumours when using points. Future work will explore rank stability of metrics, expand the pool of integrated algorithms and broaden evaluation tasks. Packaging algorithms as applications also enables future user studies to design user-realistic prompting simulations, akin to Antonov et al. [2]. Future user-studies assessing prompt placement time across different prompt types and target geometries will also be vital for effort-estimation. Lastly, future work will need to ensure that validation datasets were never used for model pre-training; this is a limitation of the proposed work and most works that build on foundation models.

**Acknowledgments.** Parhom Esmaeili is supported by the Engineering and Physical Sciences Research Council iCASE (grant number EP/Y528572/1) and co-funded by Siemens Healthineers. Virginia Fernandez is supported by NHS England.

**Disclosure of Interests.** The authors declare no competing interests to report.

# References

1. Antonelli, M., Reinke, A., Bakas, S., et al.: The medical segmentation decathlon. Nat. Commun. **13**(1), 4128 (2022). https://doi.org/10.1038/s41467-022-30695-9
2. Antonov, A., Moskalenko, A., Shepelev, D., et al.: RClicks: realistic click simulation for benchmarking interactive segmentation. In: Globerson, A., et al. (eds.) Adv. Neural Inf. Process. Syst., pp. 127673–127710. Curran Associates Inc., Vancouver (2024)
3. Boykov, Y., Jolly, M.P.: Interactive graph cuts for optimal boundary & region segmentation of objects in N-D images. In: Proceedings Eighth IEEE International Conference on Computer Vision. ICCV 2001, pp. 105–112. IEEE Comput. Soc. Vancouver (2001). https://doi.org/10.1109/ICCV.2001.937505
4. Cheng, J., et al.: SAM-Med2D (2023)
5. Du, Y., Bai, F., Huang, T., Zhao, B.: SegVol: universal and interactive volumetric medical image segmentation. In: Globerson, A., et al. (eds.) Advances in Neural Information Processing Systems, pp. 110746–110783. Curran Associates Inc., Vancouver (2024)
6. Fedorov, A., Beichel, R., Kalpathy-Cramer, J., et al.: 3D Slicer as an image computing platform for the quantitative imaging network. Mag. Resonance Imaging **30**(9), 1323–1341 (2012). https://doi.org/10.1016/j.mri.2012.05.001
7. Gatidis, S., Hepp, T., Früh, M., et al.: A whole-body FDG-PET/CT dataset with manually annotated tumor lesions. Sci. Data **9**(1), 601 (2022). https://doi.org/10.1038/s41597-022-01718-3
8. Isensee, F., Jaeger, P.F., Kohl, S.A.A., Petersen, J., Maier-Hein, K.H.: nnU-Net: a self-configuring method for deep learning-based biomedical image segmentation. Nat. Methods **18**(2), 203–211 (2021). https://doi.org/10.1038/s41592-020-01008-z
9. Isensee, F., Rokuss, M., Krämer, L., et al.: nnInteractive: redefining 3D promptable segmentation. arXiv preprint (2025)

10. Kass, M., Witkin, A., Terzopoulos, D.: Snakes: active contour models. Int. J. Comput. Vis. **1**(4), 321–331 (1988). https://doi.org/10.1007/BF00133570
11. Kirillov, A., et al.: Segment anything. arXiv preprint (2023)
12. de Kok, J.W.T.M., de la Hoz, M.A.A., de Jong, Y., et al.: A guide to sharing open healthcare data under the general data protection regulation. Sci. Data **10**(1), 404 (2023). https://doi.org/10.1038/s41597-023-02256-2
13. Lenchik, L., Heacock, L., Weaver, A.A., et al.: Automated segmentation of tissues using CT and MRI: a systematic review. Acad. Radiol. **26**(12), 1695–1706 (2019). https://doi.org/10.1016/j.acra.2019.07.006
14. Li, H., Liu, H., Hu, D., Wang, J., Oguz, I.: Prism: a promptable and robust interactive segmentation model with visual prompts. In: Linguraru, M.G., Dou, Q., Feragen, A., Giannarou, S., Glocker, B., Lekadir, K., Schnabel, J.A. (eds.) International Conference on Medical Image Computing and Computer-Assisted Intervention - MICCAI 2024, pp. 389–399. Springer, Marrakesh (2024). https://doi.org/10.1007/978-3-031-72384-1_37
15. Maier-Hein, L., Reinke, A., Godau, P., et al.: Metrics reloaded: recommendations for image analysis validation. Nat. Methods **21**(2), 195–212 (2024). https://doi.org/10.1038/s41592-023-02151-z
16. Maleki, N., Amiruddin, R., Moawad, A.W., et al.: Analysis of the MICCAI brain tumor segmentation – metastases (BraTS-METS) 2025 lighthouse challenge: brain metastasis segmentation on pre- and post-treatment MRI. arXiv preprint (2025)
17. Ravi, N., Gabeur, V., Hu, Y.T., et al.: SAM 2: segment anything in images and videos. arXiv preprint (2024)
18. Ulrich, C., Wald, T., Tempus, E., Rokuss, M., Jaeger, P.F., Maier-Hein, K.: RadioActive: 3D radiological interactive segmentation benchmark. arXiv preprint (2025)
19. Wang, H., et al.: SAM-Med3D. arXiv preprint (2023)
20. Yushkevich, P.A., et al.: User-guided 3D active contour segmentation of anatomical structures: Significantly improved efficiency and reliability. NeuroImage **31**(3), 1116–1128 (2006). https://doi.org/10.1016/j.neuroimage.2006.01.015

# Interactive Environments for Clinical Training, Education, and Human-AI Teaming

# Explainable AI for Automated User-Specific Feedback in Surgical Skill Acquisition

Catalina Gomez[1(✉)], Lalithkumar Seenivasan[1], Xinrui Zou[1], Jeewoo Yoon[1], Sirui Chu[1], Ariel Leong[2], Patrick Kramer[2], Yu-Chun Ku[1], Jose L. Porras[2], Alejandro Martin-Gomez[3], Masaru Ishii[2], and Mathias Unberath[1]

[1] Johns Hopkins University, Baltimore, MD, USA
{cgomezc1,unberath}@jhu.edu
[2] Johns Hopkins Medical Institutions, Baltimore, MD, USA
[3] University of Arkansas, Fayetteville, AR, USA

**Abstract.** Traditional surgical skill acquisition relies heavily on expert feedback, yet direct access is limited by faculty availability and variability in subjective assessments. While trainees can practice independently, the lack of personalized, objective, and quantitative feedback reduces the effectiveness of self-directed learning. Recent advances in computer vision and machine learning have enabled automated surgical skill assessment, demonstrating the feasibility of automatic competency evaluation. However, it is unclear whether such Artificial Intelligence (AI)-driven feedback can contribute to skill acquisition. Here, we examine the effectiveness of explainable AI (XAI)-generated feedback in surgical training through a human-AI study. We create a simulation-based training framework that utilizes XAI to analyze videos and extract surgical skill proxies related to primitive actions. Our intervention provides automated, user-specific feedback by comparing trainee performance to expert benchmarks and highlighting deviations from optimal execution through understandable proxies for actionable guidance. In a prospective user study with medical students, we compare the impact of XAI-guided feedback against traditional video-based coaching on task outcomes, cognitive load, and trainees' perceptions of AI-assisted learning. Results showed improved cognitive load and confidence post-intervention. While no differences emerged between the two feedback types in reducing performance gaps or practice adjustments, trends in the XAI group revealed desirable effects where participants more closely mimicked expert practice. This work encourages the study of explainable AI in surgical education and the development of data-driven, adaptive feedback mechanisms that could transform learning experiences and competency assessment.

**Keywords:** Explainable AI · Surgical training · Surgical Skill Assessment

---

C. Gomez, L. Seenivasan, X. Zou—Equal contribution.

## 1 Introduction

Surgical education faces critical constraints as limited faculty availability and persistent variability in subjective skill assessments undermine consistent, high-quality training [2]. The Accreditation Council for Graduate Medical Education's 80-hour workweek restriction, while improving the work-life balance, has reduced the time available for hands-on skill development [15]. With fewer opportunities for deliberate practice, surgical education must become more efficient without compromising competency. These challenges highlight the urgent need for scalable, objective feedback mechanisms that provide trainees with timely and actionable insights [13].

Alternative to traditional expert-based evaluation, video-based assessment has emerged as a promising tool for objectively evaluating surgical skills [10], with some programs using it to assess surgeons' readiness for independent practice [11]. However, without structured guidance, video-based assessment alone is insufficient for effective skill acquisition. The use of artificial intelligence (AI) for automated skill assessment has shown great promise [7,12]. While AI-driven assessment offers better scalability, like video-based methods, it often lacks the actionable feedback necessary to support meaningful skill improvement. Most AI solutions function as black boxes, offering overall skill ratings without providing clear, interpretable guidance [4,5,8,9,14]. To fully harness AI's potential in surgical education, it is crucial to develop systems that not only assess performance but also deliver structured, user-specific insights that facilitate skill acquisition.

Explainable AI (XAI) can address this gap by generating interpretable feedback based on measurable skill proxies—such as motion efficiency, tool trajectory, and hand stability—allowing trainees to understand their performance in a clinically relevant way [3]. By breaking down complex assessments into intuitive, actionable insights, XAI has the potential to bridge the gap between automated evaluation and real-world skill improvement. Despite its potential, limited empirical studies exist regarding whether AI-generated feedback meaningfully enhances skill development [16]. A key question remains: Can XAI effectively accelerate the acquisition of surgical skills while maintaining trainee engagement and educational value? Furthermore, the impact of AI-driven feedback on human factors, such as how trainees perceive, interpret, and integrate automated assessments, continues to be an open area of research.

In this study, we develop a simulation-based training framework that utilizes XAI to deliver user-specific, interpretable feedback for surgical skill acquisition. Through a prospective user study, we evaluate how XAI-driven feedback affects skill improvement, cognitive load, and trainees' perceptions of AI-assisted learning. By comparing this method to traditional expert demonstrations, we aim to determine whether explainable feedback offers a meaningful advantage in skill acquisition and enhancing the training experience. By aligning AI-driven feedback with principles of deliberate practice, our approach represents a step toward integrating AI-driven coaching tools into surgical training at scale.

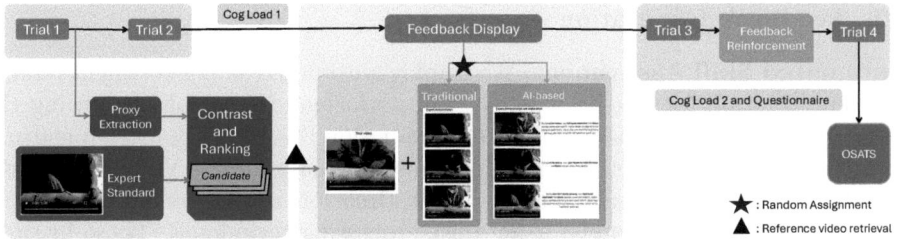

**Fig. 1.** Steps in the execution of the user study. The purple panel corresponds to the automated skill assessment and the orange one to the feedback interventions.

## 2 Methodology

### 2.1 Study Design

We design a two-arm randomized study to evaluate the effectiveness of different feedback types–XAI-generated vs traditional video-based–in teaching suturing skills in a simulation environment. XAI-generated intrinsic feedback was designed to provide user-specific guidance to improve their performance by comparing expert best practices and contrasting their execution with the maximally different primitive suturing actions. We compare this approach to traditional video-based coaching, where trainees learn through self-guided observation of expert demonstrations. We hypothesize that trainees provided with XAI feedback will show greater improvements in the targeted skill concepts and enhanced perceptions of AI-assisted learning.

The experimental task emulated wound closure procedures with four interrupted instrument-tied sutures using a needle driver, surgical forceps, and suture scissors in incisions made on a skin suturing board [6]. Each suturing board was divided into quadrants. To standardize incision orientation and suture placement, participants always worked in the top-left quadrant and placed the first suture at the furthest end of the incision. Video recordings were captured using an Intel RealSense D435i RGBD sensor, though only RGB data was used for processing. We recruited 12 medical students with previous exposure to suturing and randomly assigned them to one of the two feedback interventions.

In our study (Fig. 1), participants completed four trials across two sessions, with a feedback intervention between sessions. The first session was followed by the cognitive load assessment and a break. We randomly assigned participants to a feedback type and gave a fixed time for feedback interpretation. In the second session, the same feedback was presented again before the last trial to reinforce its effect. This session concluded with another cognitive load assessment and feedback on perceptions. Last, participants viewed two of their trial videos (the second of each session) and rated their skills using a condensed global average rating scale (OSATS).

## 2.2 Feedback Generation

**Automated Skill Assessment:** We employ automated skill assessment to analyze hand motion for fine-grained surgical performance analysis. Following the approach in [3], we first perform gesture prediction based on the motion features extracted using object detection and 2D pose estimation. The YOLOX-S model detects hands and surgical tools. A pose estimation model predicts hand keypoints, which are then refined using post-processing techniques. These features serve as input for the MSTCN++ model, which classifies gestures into six categories: "No Gesture," "Needle Passing (G1)," "Pull The Suture (G2)," "Instrumental Tie (G3)," "Lay The Knot (G4)," and "Cut The Suture (G5)," based on the open surgery simulation dataset [6]. Here, we use the pre-trained models from [3]. We then calculate the proxies for each detected gesture to quantify interpretable surgical action primitives. These proxies provide quantitative measures of hand pose characteristics relevant to skill assessment, using measurements previously identified as clinically relevant to analyze motion features [3].

- **Hand Orientation (HO):** This proxy measures how much the hand is turned. High values mean the palm is facing down (pronated), values near zero mean the hand is sideways, and low values mean the palm is facing up (supinated). Clinically, appropriate hand orientation is crucial for executing precise surgical movements. For instance, a slightly supinated hand can help achieve an optimal cutting angle when severing a suture [3].
- **Distance between Thumb and Index finger (DF):** This proxy measures the space between the tips of the thumb and index finger and reflects different ways of holding tools and sutures. Surgeons typically secure the needle driver by resting it in the palm and grip sutures with their fingertips for precision, while novices rely on less refined grips that favor stability over accuracy [3].

**Expert Data Collection:** We collected expert data ($N = 5$) under the same experimental setup to establish a benchmark for skill. Experts completed four trials, performing four sutures per trial. These samples were processed using the gesture prediction and proxy calculation pipeline described above. To accurately calculate the proxies, we used the model-predicted hand poses and tools detection, and manually annotated surgical gestures. For each gesture, we computed the corresponding proxy values over time. Then, we average these values for each proxy-gesture pair $(c - g)$ with $c = \{\text{RHO, LHO, RDF, LDF}\}$ and $g = \{\text{G1, G2, G3, G4, G5}\}$, as $P = \frac{1}{n}\sum_{t=1}^{n} p_t$, where $p_t$ is the proxy value at time $t$. To establish a "standard" proxy-gesture pair representing typical expert performance, we combined values across experts over multiple trials:

$$P_{ref} = \frac{1}{N \times T} \sum_{j=1}^{N} \sum_{i=1}^{T} P_{j,i} \qquad (1)$$

where, $N = 5$ experts, $T = 4$ trials, and $P_{j,i}$ is the average proxy value for expert $j$ at trial $i$.

Using these expert-derived standard values, we selected video segments that best matched the standard proxy-gesture pairs. We created two formats of the retrieved video to align with different feedback paradigms. For the traditional feedback condition, we provided a reference video showing a complete suture placement as a broad learning resource. For the XAI feedback, we curated video fragments, each focusing on a specific gesture related to the proxy measurement, serving as a more targeted exemplar of the proxy.

**Feedback Presentation Through the User Interface:** We processed each participant's first trial ($P_{j,1}$) to provide real-time feedback intervention after the first session. To manage the information load during the intervention, we selected a subset of proxy-gesture combinations. For each participant, we first calculated the absolute difference between the average proxy value for each gesture and the corresponding expert standard, namely $P_{j,1} - P_{ref}$ for each $(c, g)$ pair, following the strategy to compare a new sample to the average of experts [3]. We then selected the top three differences with the largest deviations. We developed a custom user interface to present this feedback, including a self-video recording for comparison and recall, specifically the participant's second suture from the first trial that was used to generate the feedback. For both interventions, we presented expert demonstrations for the top three proxy-gesture pairs, i.e., either a full suture demonstration or a video clip focusing on the specific gesture related to the proxy. The explainable feedback intervention included explicit guidance next to each expert video, following this template: "During [gesture], your [hand] [proxy name] had [relative position] average values than experts."

## 2.3 Measures, Data Analysis and Statistics

We report proxy values for the proxy-gesture pairs (included in the feedback intervention) for the $2^{nd}$ and $4^{th}$ trials. To accurately capture potential changes from the feedback intervention, we manually annotated the gestures for all sutures in these trials. First, to quantify the performance gap with experts, we calculate the relative difference at the $i^{th}$ trial for the $j^{th}$ participant as: $S_{j,i} = |P_{j,i} - P_{ref}|/P_{ref}$. We then measured improvement by calculating the difference between performance gaps in the second and fourth trials. Second, we quantify the relative change of the proxy values before and after the intervention by calculating the difference in the proxy measurements for each participant. Cognitive load was assessed using the NASA TLX questionnaire (mental and physical demand, performance, effort, and frustration). Participants also rated their confidence in performing sutures on a ten-point scale and feedback usefulness and their understanding using a five-point Likert scale [1]. We displayed two video clips from each participant for a self-evaluation using a simplified OSATS. For ordinal data from the survey responses, we used a non-parametric two-way Analysis of Variance (ANOVA) for session and feedback type comparisons, and independent t-tests (or a MannWhitney U test if assumptions are unmet) for continuous variables to be compared across feedback types.

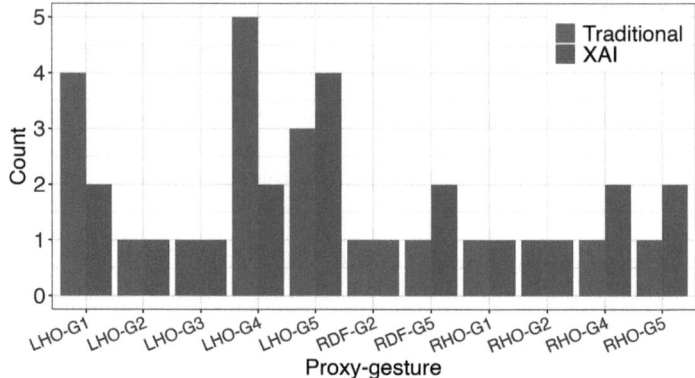

**Fig. 2.** Distribution of the top-three proxy-gesture pairs that had the largest deviations in the first trial and were presented to participants at each group.

## 3 Results

**a) Change in the Relative Gap Between Participants' Proxy Measurements and Expert Standards with Different Feedback:**

Figure 2 shows the distribution of the top-three proxy-gesture pairs that had the largest deviations in the first trial and were used for the feedback intervention, representing the specific proxy measurements on which we quantified relative gaps. We measured the difference in the relative gap for the top-three concepts before and after the feedback intervention, and averaged those differences into a single measurement per participant (Fig. 3 left). The traditional feedback group showed an average change of 0.55 ($SD = 0.94, CI : [-0.44, 1.54]$), while the XAI feedback group showed an average change of $-0.46$ ($SD = 1.77, CI : [-2.32, 1.40]$). The positive change suggests that participants in the traditional group moved further from expert standards, while the negative value shows that XAI feedback helped participants move closer. However, the difference was not significant ($t(7.6) = 1.23, p = 0.254$).

**b) Change in Proxy Measurements Before and After Different Feedback Interventions:**

For each of the top-three ranked proxy-gesture pairs, we calculated the relative change before and after presenting the feedback and averaged these change values for each participant (Fig. 3 right). On average, the relative change in proxy measurements was larger in the traditional group ($M = 0.54, SD = 0.60, CI : [-0.09, 1.17]$) than the XAI group ($M = 0.37, SD = 0.29, CI : [0.02, 0.73]$), but not significantly ($W = 16, p = 0.927$). Unlike the traditional group, the average relative change in the XAI group was significantly different from zero, indicating measurable proxy value changes after receiving explainable feedback.

**c) Impact of Feedback Interventions on Subjective Measurements:** The feedback type did not significantly affect participants' cognitive load ($F(1, 10) =$

$0.40, p = 0.540$), with an average of 4.07 ($SD = 1.19$) and 4.50 ($SD = 0.86$) in the traditional and XAI groups, respectively. However, session progression showed a significant effect ($F(1, 10) = 7.80, p = 0.019$), with cognitive load decreasing from before ($M = 4.63, SD = 1.13$) to after the feedback intervention ($M = 3.93, SD = 0.84$), regardless of the information presented. No significant interaction effect between feedback type and session was observed ($F(1, 10) = 0.09, p = 0.770$). For perceived usefulness (Cronbach's $\alpha = 0.92$), participants in the XAI group rated it slightly higher ($M = 3.67, SD = 0.98$) than those in the traditional group ($M = 3.42, SD = 0.67$). However, this difference was not significant ($W = 15, p = 0.677$). For perceived understanding (Cronbach's $\alpha = 0.74$), both groups reported the same average rating ($M = 3.58$), but variability was higher in the XAI group ($SD = 0.86$) compared to the traditional group ($SD = 0.38$). This comparison was also non-significant ($W = 15, p = 0.672$).

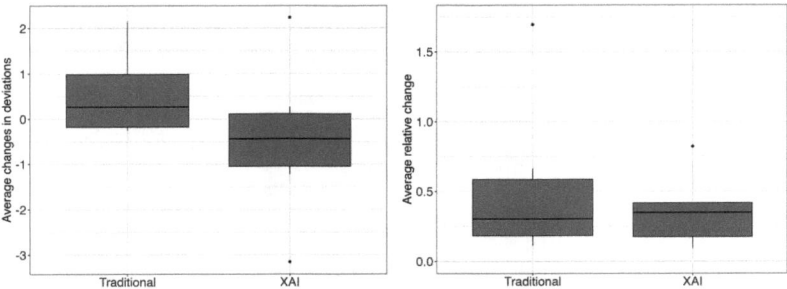

**Fig. 3.** Box and whisker plots for average change in deviations with respect to experts and average relative change in proxy values for the top three.

Feedback type had no significant effect on participants' confidence ($F(1, 10) = 0.24, p = 0.632$), with the traditional feedback group reporting slightly higher confidence ($M = 4.33, SD = 1.92$) than the XAI feedback group ($M = 4.17, SD = 1.27$). Regardless of feedback type, participants felt significantly more confident after the training intervention ($M = 4.92, SD = 1.44$) than before ($M = 3.58, SD = 1.50$), $F(1, 10) = 11.72, p = 0.007$. The interaction effect was not significant ($F(1, 10) = 0.13, p = 0.725$). Among the perceived competence constructs, only instrument handling showed a significant effect of session progression ($F(1, 10) = 5.79, p = 0.037$), with ratings increasing from before ($M = 2.50, SD = 0.80$) to after ($M = 3.00, SD = 0.85$). There was no significant effect of feedback type on this competence ($F(1, 10) = 0.24, P = 0.633$) with participants in the traditional feedback group rating on average 2.58 ($SD = 1.00$) and in the XAI group reporting a slightly higher self-assessment ($M = 2.92, SD = 0.67$). The interaction effect was not significant ($F(1, 10) = 0.24, p = 0.632$).

**d) Qualitative Results:** Given the promising results of the XAI feedback intervention in moving participants closer to expert standards, we manually reviewed cases that showed notable improvements in reducing relative gaps among the top three concepts. Figure 4 shows samples from video clips of participants before and after feedback, alongside expert demonstrations for each proxy-gesture pair. In the first example, the average RDF was below the experts' average. After receiving XAI feedback, the participant adjusted closer to the experts' standards, resulting in a greater DF. The second and third (rows) examples illustrate the RHO during different gestures: laying the knot and pulling the sutures. The expert clip shows that a less pronated hand position is needed, requiring a reduction in the participants' proxy measurement. Following the intervention, the participant successfully reduced their average proxy values and began using the needle driver to pull the suture, aligning more closely with the expert's technique.

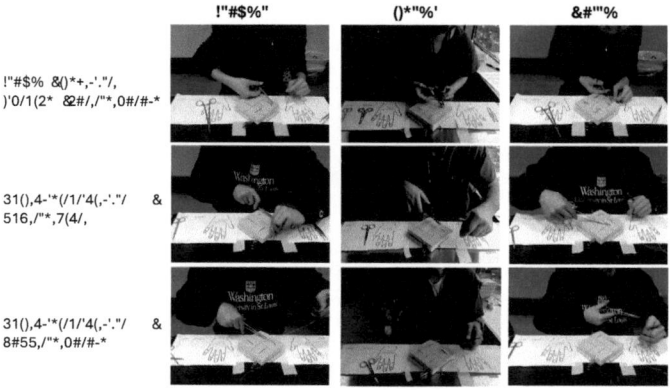

**Fig. 4.** Video clips from participants in the XAI group that showed less deviation from expert standards after receiving explained expert feedback.

## 4  Discussion and Conclusion

We present a novel implementation of AI-assisted methods for surgical skill training, with XAI providing near real-time personalized and interpretable feedback. Our initial findings did not demonstrate the superiority of XAI-generated feedback over traditional training methods in aligning performance with expert standards or shaping participant perceptions using statistical tests. We believe that this is for various reasons, that we will discuss separately below. Regardless, the large variations we observed in our measurements, compounded with the relatively small sample size, we believe that our results have to be interpreted with care. Furthermore, while we used averaged proxy values for aggregating an individual's practice, the underlying concepts may exhibit temporal variation within each gesture, suggesting that temporal analyses could provide more meaningful comparisons between expert and novice performance. Nevertheless, we did find positive trends both in quantitative and qualitative analyses, which we believe warrants further investigation of these XAI-based interventions in skill training.

The substantial deviations from expert standards indicate potential areas for improvement; however, the skillset of our participants with little surgical exposure may affect learning and their capacity to benefit from the intervention. The value of advanced feedback for transforming novices into experts appears limited when learners are still mastering fundamental skills and four trials may be insufficient to observe meaningful changes. Notably, participants in both feedback groups reported similar increases in confidence over time and comparable feedback usefulness, suggesting that early-stage learners may focus more on gaining general task familiarity rather than responding differently to specific feedback formats. While participants may gain insights from feedback interventions, as shown in the qualitative examples with the desirable effect of XAI feedback, translating these insights into improved practice remains challenging for novices.

We identified methodological constraints in our intervention design that may have affected its effectiveness. The brief, single-trial feedback intervention was limited by real-time processing requirements and study duration. Moreover, our automated skill assessment uses existing out-of-the-box models [3], pre-trained with its own experts and novice samples. Variations in surgical environments, lighting, or tool occlusions may affect detection, leading to gesture misclassification and unreliable proxies. The proxy calculations use pixel coordinates without depth information, potentially introducing errors in motion analysis, and the frontal view limits the capture of hand movements and tool interactions. Future implementations would benefit from adaptable models with improved robustness, depth estimation capabilities, and multi-view analysis to enhance spatial accuracy and provide more reliable feedback for effective skill assessment.

Incorporating understandable, task-specific feedback mechanisms with AI can automate the guidance of trainees toward expert-level performance. By identifying which aspects of AI-assisted learning support skill acquisition more effectively, we can iteratively improve these interventions to better align with the needs of trainees and develop human-centered AI for surgical education.

**Acknowledgements.** This study was funded by the Johns Hopkins DELTA Grant IO 80061108 and the Link Foundation Fellowship in Modeling, Simulation, and Training.

# References

1. Alameddine, M.B., Englesbe, M.J., Waits, S.A.: A video-based coaching intervention to improve surgical skill in fourth-year medical students. J. Surg. Educ. **75**(6), 1475–1479 (2018)
2. Babineau, T.J., et al.: The cost of operative training for surgical residents. Arch. Surg. **139**(4), 366–370 (2004)
3. Bkheet, E., D'Angelo, A.L., Goldbraikh, A., Laufer, S.: Using hand pose estimation to automate open surgery training feedback. Int. J. Comput. Assist. Radiol. Surg. **18**(7), 1279–1285 (2023)

4. Funke, I., Mees, S.T., Weitz, J., Speidel, S.: Video-based surgical skill assessment using 3d convolutional neural networks. Int. J. Comput. Assist. Radiol. Surg. **14**, 1217–1225 (2019)
5. Ghasemloonia, A., Maddahi, Y., Zareinia, K., Lama, S., Dort, J.C., Sutherland, G.R.: Surgical skill assessment using motion quality and smoothness. J. Surg. Educ. **74**(2), 295–305 (2017)
6. Goldbraikh, A., Volk, T., Pugh, C.M., Laufer, S.: Using open surgery simulation kinematic data for tool and gesture recognition. Int. J. Comput. Assist. Radiol. Surg. 1–15 (2022). https://doi.org/10.1007/s11548-022-02615-1
7. Kirubarajan, A., Young, D., Khan, S., Crasto, N., Sobel, M., Sussman, D.: Artificial intelligence and surgical education: a systematic scoping review of interventions. J. Surg. Educ. **79**(2), 500–515 (2022)
8. Lavanchy, J.L., et al.: Automation of surgical skill assessment using a three-stage machine learning algorithm. Sci. Rep. **11**(1), 5197 (2021)
9. Liu, D., et al.: Towards unified surgical skill assessment. In: Proceedings of the IEEE/CVF Conference on Computer Vision and Pattern Recognition, pp. 9522–9531 (2021)
10. Mackenzie, C.F., et al.: Head-camera video recordings of trauma core competency procedures can evaluate surgical resident's technical performance as well as colocated evaluators. J. Trauma Acute Care Surg. **83**(1), S124–S129 (2017)
11. Miskovic, D., Wyles, S.M., Carter, F., Coleman, M.G., Hanna, G.B.: Development, validation and implementation of a monitoring tool for training in laparoscopic colorectal surgery in the English national training program. Surg. Endosc. **25**, 1136–1142 (2011)
12. Patel, V.L., et al.: The coming of age of artificial intelligence in medicine. Artif. Intell. Med. **46**(1), 5–17 (2009)
13. Scott, D.J.: Patient safety, competency, and the future of surgical simulation. Simul. Healthcare **1**(3), 164–170 (2006)
14. Wang, Z., Majewicz Fey, A.: Deep learning with convolutional neural network for objective skill evaluation in robot-assisted surgery. Int. J. Comput. Assist. Radiol. Surg. **13**(12), 1959–1970 (2018). https://doi.org/10.1007/s11548-018-1860-1
15. Wilson, M.R.: The new ACGME resident duty hours: big changes, bigger challenges. Ochsner J. **5**(2), 3–5 (2003)
16. Yilmaz, R., et al.: Real-time multifaceted artificial intelligence vs in-person instruction in teaching surgical technical skills: a randomized controlled trial. Sci. Rep. **14**(1), 15130 (2024)

# Real-Time, Dynamic, and Highly Generalizable Ultrasound Image Simulation-Guided Procedure Training System for Musculoskeletal Minimally Invasive Treatment

Xiandi Wang[1](✉), Zekun Jiang[2], Mengqi Tang[1], Ying Han[1], Dan Pu[1], and Kang Li[2](✉)

[1] Medical Simulation Center of West China Hospital, Sichuan University, Chengdu Sichuan 610000, China
wxdfrank@scu.edu.cn

[2] West China Biomedical Big Data Center, West China Hospital, Sichuan University, Chengdu Sichuan 610000, China
orthoxiao@gmail.com

**Abstract.** Ultrasound-guided musculoskeletal minimally invasive procedures offer clear clinical benefits, yet remain technically challenging to master. Existing deep learning-based ultrasound simulation methods often focus on static, fixed-plane images, lacking real-time and dynamic capabilities essential for clinical training. To address this, we propose RDG-USIS: a Real-time, Dynamic, and Generalizable UltraSound Image Simulation algorithm designed to enhance training for minimally invasive procedures. We first introduce a CT-ultrasound data acquisition method with 3D spatial constraints, generating paired CT-ultrasound data by resampling CT volumes according to ultrasound probe pose. RDG-USIS consists of two stages: structural segmentation using a Total-Segmentator based on nnU-Net, followed by ultrasound simulation via an improved convolutional ray-casting algorithm. A CycleGAN model then translates the simulated images into realistic ultrasound style, trained using both synthetic and real data. We benchmark RDG-USIS against Pix2Pix and Diffusion models, and conduct ablation studies. The results show superior structural accuracy and visual realism. Finally, the model is integrated into a multi-modal training system and evaluated in clinical tasks, confirming its real-time performance and generalizability. The source code is available at https://github.com/JZK00/RDG-USIS.

**Keywords:** Ultrasound Image Simulation · Procedure Training System · Style Transfer · Deep Generative Models

---

X. Wang and Z. Jiang—These authors contributed equally to this work.

## 1 Introduction

Musculoskeletal ultrasound-guided procedures, such as spine injections and nerve blocks, are widely used in orthopedics, pain management, and sports medicine [4]. Compared to blind or X-ray-guided techniques, ultrasound provides real-time visualization, greater flexibility, and no radiation exposure. However, these procedures require precise needle control, spatial reasoning, and skilled probe handling [3,12], making training time-consuming-especially in freehand operations where landmarks constantly shift.

To enhance training, an intelligent ultrasound-guided system that mimics real clinical dynamics is essential. High-quality simulation is central to this goal. An effective system must reproduce both the visual style and spatial imaging characteristics defined by tissue and probe position [5,13]. Current methods face limitations: physics-based simulations lack realism, while deep learning approaches struggle with real-time dynamics [9,10].

The key challenges lie in data acquisition, algorithm design, and validation. Most prior studies use static, fixed-plane data [14], limiting dynamic simulation across patients and views. Diffusion models [8,15,16] are too slow, and GANs [11,14] often fail to retain probe-related artifacts. Few systems undergo full clinical deployment.

To address these gaps, we propose **RDG-USIS**, a **R**eal-time, **D**ynamic, and **G**eneralizable **U**ltra**S**ound **I**mage **S**imulation framework embedded in a training system. It introduces innovations in imaging acquisition, simulation, and validation. Our main contributions are summarized as follows.

1. We propose a CT-ultrasound acquisition method with 3D spatial constraints for aligned datasets.
2. We present a simulation algorithm preserving both style and structure, including probe artifacts.
3. We demonstrate that the integration of physical simulation and generative models for better realism and generalization.
4. We implement clinical validation in free-hand procedures, confirming real-time and cross-subject performance.

## 2 Methods

We first outline the workflow of our method in Fig. 1, covering data acquisition, RDG-USIS algorithm development, and deployment for clinical validation. Each component is detailed below.

### 2.1 CT-Ultrasound Image Acquisition

To build a high-quality dataset, we designed a system ensuring anatomical consistency between CT and ultrasound. As shown in Fig. 1A, the system includes a CT scanner, optical tracker, position calibration tools, and a handheld ultrasound device.

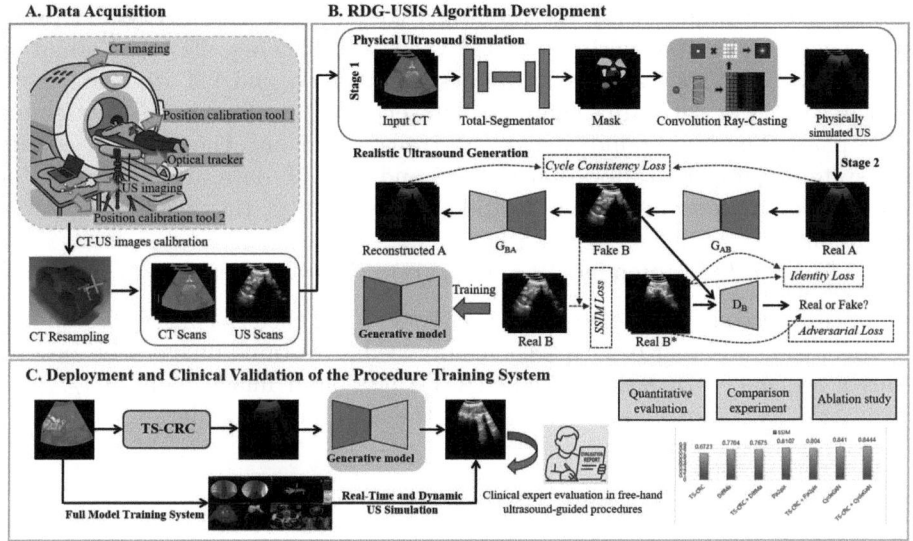

**Fig. 1. Overall Workflow of Our Study.** (A) CT-Ultrasound imaging data acquisition method with three-dimensional spatial constraints. (B) The RDG-USIS algorithm is developed, including two stages of ultrasound simulation. (C) We deploy RDG-USIS into a multi-modal training system and implement clinical evaluations.

**Imaging Acquisition System.** A custom 3D-printed reference frame with four steel balls is attached to the subject and captured in the CT scan. This frame enables spatial registration via rigid transformation calculated using the SVD method [1]. Given four corresponding points in the CT coordinate $\{P_i^{CT}\}$ and in tracker coordinates $\{P_i^{Tracker}\}$, we solve for the rigid transformation $T_{CT \to Tracker} = [R|t]$, where $R \in SO(3)$, $t \in R^3$, by minimizing:

$$\min_{R,t} \sum_{i=1}^{4} \left\| R \cdot \boldsymbol{p}_i^{CT} + \boldsymbol{t} - \boldsymbol{p}_i^{Traker} \right\|^2 \tag{1}$$

An optical tracker records the 6-DOF pose of the ultrasound probe using reflective markers, enabling synchronized frame acquisition.

**CT Imaging and Processing.** Subjects undergo a CT scan while wearing the tracker. After reconstruction, we segment and align the steel balls to compute the CT-to-tracker transformation. We then resample CT slices according to ultrasound probe poses. For a given ultrasound frame at probe pose $T_{Probe}^k$, the corresponding CT slice is generated by:

$$I_{CT}^k = \text{Resample}\left(V_{CT}, T_{Probe}^k \cdot T_{CT \to Tracker}\right) \tag{2}$$

where $V_{CT}$ is the CT volume, and $I_{CT}^k$ is the k-th resampled CT slice in the ultrasound probe orientation.

**Ultrasound Imaging and Rendering.** We calibrate the ultrasound probe using a water phantom with N-shaped wires, establishing the transformation from image pixels to tracker coordinates. Ultrasound and CT data are registered in 3D Slicer software. The final dataset contains aligned CT-Ultrasound image pairs. The ultrasound images are transformed into the tracking coordinate system using the calibration matrix, and the CT data are aligned to the same coordinate system via the position tracker $T_{Probe}^{k}$, thus achieving spatial unification.

$$I_{CT}^{k} = \text{Render}\left(V_{CT}, T_{Probe}^{k}\right), \quad I_{US}^{k} = \text{Frame}(k) \qquad (3)$$

For each recorded probe pose $I_{US}^{k}$, we render a CT slice $I_{CT}^{k}$ in the corresponding orientation and pair it with the synchronized ultrasound image. This process yields a sequence of spatially aligned CT-Ultrasound image pairs $(I_{CT}^{k}, I_{US}^{k})$, which serve as standard data for training the ultrasound simulation model.

## 2.2 RDG-USIS Algorithm Development

RDG-USIS is an ultrasound simulation framework that combines physical modeling with generative models (Fig. 1B). The framework consists of two main stages: Stage 1 performs physical ultrasound image simulation based on anatomical structures and acoustic modeling (named TS-CRC), while Stage 2 employs a generative adversarial network for ultrasound style translation to achieve highly realistic ultrasound image generation.

**Physical Ultrasound Simulation.** First, we segment 3D CT using the TotalSegmentator based on nnU-Net [6,18] to automatically extract structural regions corresponding to muscle, bone, and fat. Each tissue is modeled with five acoustic parameters: sound speed, acoustic impedance, attenuation coefficient, scatterer density, and scatterer intensity. Then, the TS-CRC algorithm performs ray-based simulation, generating the simulated B-mode images with post-processing: speckle noise, TGC, compression, and scan conversion. The detailed algorithmic information is provided in the GitHub repository.

**Realistic Ultrasound Generation.** The TS-CRC algorithm can generate simulated ultrasound images with physically realistic tissue structures, but the visual style still differs from real ultrasound. To enhance visual realism, we introduce a CycleGAN model [19] to learn a mapping between the simulated images and real ultrasound images. During the generative model training, the model is optimized using a combination of loss functions: $L_{GAN}$, $L_{cyc}$, $L_{id}$, and $L_{SSIM}$.

Here, we add the structural similarity loss $L_{SSIM}$, which is introduced to enhance the preservation of anatomical structure during translation. So, the final training objective is defined as:

$$L_{Total} = L_{GAN} + \gamma_1 L_{cyc} + \gamma_2 L_{id} + \gamma_3 L_{SSIM} \qquad (4)$$

where $\gamma_1$, $\gamma_2$, and $\gamma_3$ are weighting coefficients controlling the balance among the different losses.

This method effectively translates the physically simulated ultrasound images generated by TS-CRC into high-quality ultrasound images with a visual style closely matching that of real ultrasound, while preserving detailed anatomical structures across various tissue regions.

### 2.3 System Deployment and Clinical Validation

We deploy RDG-USIS in a multi-modal surgical training system, called Full Modal Training System (Fig. 1C). Real-time probe pose controls ultrasound simulation alongside CT and DR visualization.

**Qualitative and Quantitative Evaluation.** We comprehensively evaluate the ultrasound simulation performance of RDG-USIS from both qualitative and quantitative perspectives. On both validation and test sets, we compare RDG-USIS with baseline methods including pix2pix [7], TS-CRC + pix2pix, DiffMa [17], and TS-CRC + DiffMa. Quantitative metrics, including MSE, PSNR, SSIM, and FID, are used to assess image similarity. Meanwhile, we conduct ablation studies to evaluate the contribution of different algorithmic components. Additionally, expert ultrasound physicians visually review and score the simulated outputs.

**Prospective Clinical Evaluation.** We further evaluate RDG-USIS in the real-time, cross-subject musculoskeletal minimally invasive treatment training settings with clinical experts. Criteria include anatomical consistency and ultrasound style preservation. The evaluation uses a custom training platform integrating our simulation system, a physical lumbar phantom (3D-printed spine, foam, skin), and an electromagnetic tracking setup. CT data from a digital human not in the training set ensures generalization. Experts interact with a

**Table 1. Method Comparison Results.** We show MSE, PSNR, SSIM, FID, and the run time (s) measured across different ultrasound image simulation methods. The values are the average of all scans in the test set.

| Medels | Methods | MSE | PSNR | SSIM | FID | Times(s) |
|---|---|---|---|---|---|---|
| Model-1 | TS-CRC | 36.415 | 32.575 | 0.672 | 243.120 | 0.216 |
| Model-2 | DiffMa | 24.216 | 34.404 | 0.770 | 14.493 | 0.565 |
| Model-3 | TS-CRC + DiffMa | 24.434 | 34.359 | 0.767 | 16.321 | 0.781 |
| Model-4 | Pix2Pix | 22.746 | 34.671 | 0.810 | **6.033** | **0.040** |
| Model-5 | TS-CRC + Pix2Pix | 23.162 | 34.593 | 0.804 | 6.997 | 0.256 |
| Model-6 | CycleGAN | **22.090** | **34.802** | 0.841 | 24.045 | 0.090 |
| **Ours** | **TS-CRC + CycleGAN** | 22.514 | 34.725 | **0.844** | 15.999 | 0.306 |

mock probe and view real-time outputs. Structured scoring covers anatomy, realism, and style fidelity, confirming simulation accuracy and clinical relevance.

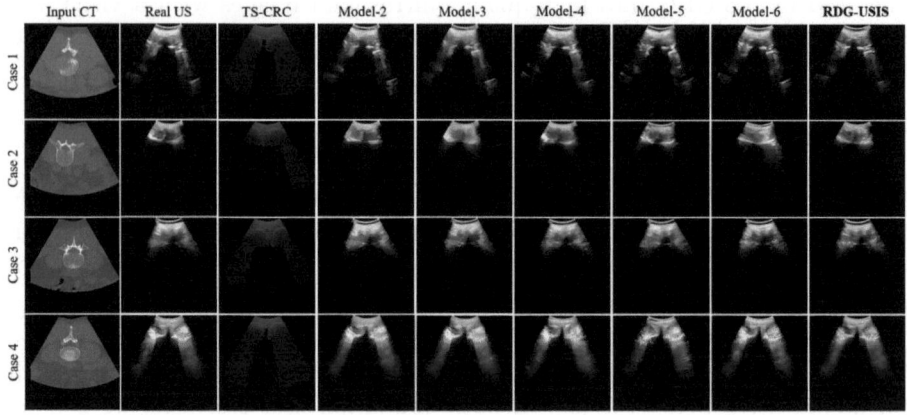

**Fig. 2. Comparison of Ultrasound Image Simulation Results in the Test Set.** Visualization examples include input CT, real ultrasound, and various simulated ultrasound outputs. RDG-USIS, along with several other models, demonstrates performance that closely approximates real ultrasound images.

## 3 Results

### 3.1 CT-Ultrasound Datasets

Our study was approved by the institutional ethics committee of West China Hospital, and informed consent was obtained from all participants. In total, the study includes 11,254 CT-ultrasound scan pairs in the training set, 3,523 pairs in the validation set, and 1,771 pairs in an independent external test set. In the prospective evaluation based on a digital human model, experts freely conducted real-time simulation and observation without a fixed data quantity. The training set was used to develop the generative models, while comparative analysis and evaluation were performed on the validation and test sets.

**Table 2. Ablation Study of RDG-USIS.** The values are the average of all scans in the test set.

| TS-CRC | CycleGAN(Ori) | CycleGAN(SSIM) | MSE | PSNR | SSIM | FID |
|---|---|---|---|---|---|---|
| Yes | | | 36.415 | 32.575 | 0.672 | 243.122 |
| | Yes | | 38.373 | 32.322 | 0.628 | 51.589 |
| | Yes | Yes | **22.090** | **34.802** | 0.841 | 24.045 |
| Yes | Yes | | 32.437 | 33.081 | 0.667 | 70.167 |
| **Yes** | **Yes** | **Yes** | 22.514 | 34.725 | **0.844** | **15.999** |

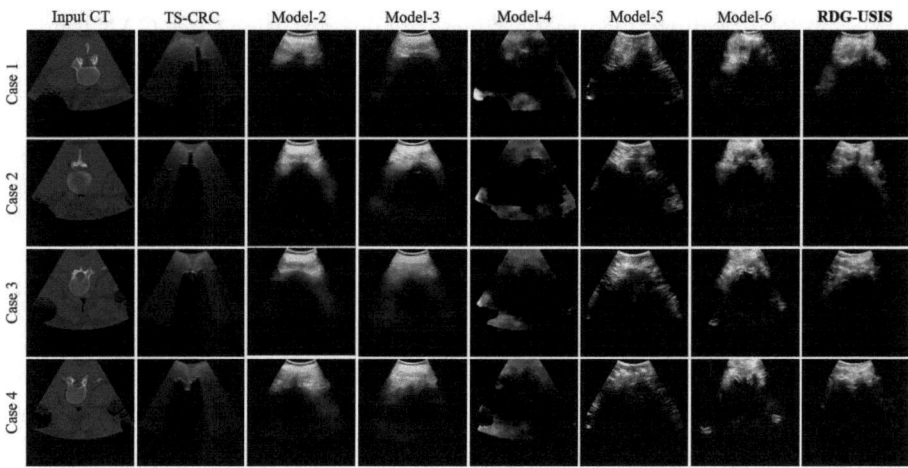

**Fig. 3. Comparison of Ultrasound Image Simulation Results in the Prospective Evaluation Set.** RDG-USIS outperforms other models in realism.

### 3.2 Qualitative and Quantitative Evaluation of RDG-USIS

First, we comprehensively evaluate the ultrasound simulation performance of RDG-USIS in the test set. Table 1 and Figs. 2 present the evaluation metrics and visual comparisons of different ultrasound generation models. RDG-USIS achieves the top SSIM and strong FID scores.

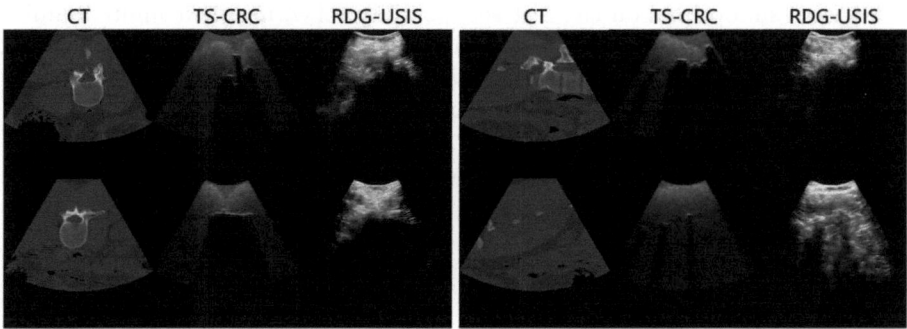

**Fig. 4. Ultrasound Simulation Performance of RDG-USIS Across Different CT Planes.** RDG-USIS shows strong cross-subject and cross-plane performance.

In the subsequent prospective evaluation (see Fig. 3), RDG-USIS demonstrates clear advantages, with the best preservation of anatomical structures and ultrasound style. Other models, such as pix2pix, achieve the best FID but perform poorly in generalization evaluation, showing structural inconsistencies.

DiffMa model introduces incorrect artifacts, while only using CycleGAN tends to miss critical details. Furthermore, in cross-subject and cross-plane tests, our method also demonstrates strong ultrasound simulation and generalization performance (Fig. 4).

The ablation study in Table 2 further confirms the effectiveness of components such as TS-CRC and CycleGAN SSIM loss in improving simulation performance.

### 3.3 Clinical Validation of Our Full Modal Training System

We invited three musculoskeletal ultrasound and orthopedic experts from different hospital centers to participate in the user study and evaluation. Each expert has more than 15 years of clinical practice experience. Three experts scored our system across four criteria (each on a 5-point scale), averaging 4.3 (anatomical), 4.0 (usability), 3.7 (noise/artifact), and 3.3 (realism). The dynamic video demonstration of our training system is provided in the Materials.

## 4 Discussion and Conclusion

We proposed RDG-USIS, a real-time, dynamic, and generalizable ultrasound simulation algorithm, integrated into a training system for minimally invasive procedures. The system improves training quality and outperforms existing generative models in clinical use, though some limitations remain. First, occasional simulation failures likely stem from limited training data in the mid-spine region. While structural alignment was preserved, style transfer was less effective. Increasing data diversity may enhance robustness. Second, metrics like MSE and PSNR were suboptimal on the test set, possibly reflecting their limited clinical relevance [2] or areas needing model refinement. Lastly, the evaluation involved only three experts. Wider deployment and broader feedback in clinical training environments are needed to further improve and validate the system.

**Disclosure of Interests.** The authors have no competing interests to declare that are relevant to the content of this article.

## References

1. Andrews, H., Patterson, C.: Singular value decomposition (SVD) image coding. IEEE Trans. Commun. **24**(4), 425–432 (2003)
2. Boumeridja, H., et al.: Enhancing fetal ultrasound image quality and anatomical plane recognition in low-resource settings using super-resolution models. Sci. Rep. **15**(1), 8376 (2025)
3. Cipolletta, E., et al.: Ultrasound-guided procedures in rheumatology daily practice: feasibility, accuracy, and safety issues. JCR: J. Clinic. Rheumat. **27**(6), 226–231 (2021)
4. Daftary, A.R., Karnik, A.S.: Perspectives in ultrasound-guided musculoskeletal interventions. Indian J. Radiol. Imaging **25**(03), 246–260 (2015)

5. Hu, Y., et al.: Freehand ultrasound image simulation with spatially-conditioned generative adversarial networks. In: International Workshop on Computational Methods for Molecular Imaging, pp. 105–115. Springer (2017)
6. Isensee, F., Jaeger, P.F., Kohl, S.A., Petersen, J., Maier-Hein, K.H.: NNU-Net: a self-configuring method for deep learning-based biomedical image segmentation. Nat. Methods **18**(2), 203–211 (2021)
7. Isola, P., Zhu, J.Y., Zhou, T., Efros, A.A.: Image-to-image translation with conditional adversarial networks. In: Proceedings of the IEEE Conference on Computer Vision and Pattern Recognition, pp. 1125–1134 (2017)
8. Katakis, S., et al.: Generation of musculoskeletal ultrasound images with diffusion models. BioMedInformatics **3**(2), 405–421 (2023)
9. Li, A., Han, J., Zhao, Y., Li, K., Liu, L.: Realistic ultrasound synthesis based on diagnostic CT to facilitate ultrasound-guided robotic spine surgery. IEEE Trans. Med. Robot. Bionics **5**(4), 879–889 (2023)
10. Li, K., Mao, X., Ye, C., Li, A., Xu, Y., Meng, M.Q.H.: Style transfer enabled sim2real framework for efficient learning of robotic ultrasound image analysis using simulated data. arXiv preprint arXiv:2305.09169 (2023)
11. Liang, J., et al.: Sketch guided and progressive growing GAN for realistic and editable ultrasound image synthesis. Med. Image Anal. **79**, 102461 (2022)
12. Maddali, D., Brun, H., Kiss, G., Hjelmervik, J.M., Elle, O.J.: Spatial orientation in cardiac ultrasound images using mixed reality: design and evaluation. Front. Virt. Reality **3**, 881338 (2022)
13. Magnetti, C., et al.: Deep generative models to simulate 2D patient-specific ultrasound images in real time. In: Annual Conference on Medical Image Understanding and Analysis, pp. 423–435. Springer (2020)
14. Song, Y., Chong, N.Y.: S-CycleGAN: semantic segmentation enhanced CT-ultrasound image-to-image translation for robotic ultrasonography. In: 2024 IEEE International Conference on Cyborg and Bionic Systems (CBS), pp. 115–120. IEEE (2024)
15. Song, Z., Zhou, Y., Wang, J., Ma, C.Z.H., Zheng, Y.: Synthesizing real-time ultrasound images of muscle based on biomechanical simulation and conditional diffusion network. Ferroelectrics, and Frequency Control, IEEE Transactions on Ultrasonics (2024)
16. Stojanovski, D., Hermida, U., Lamata, P., Beqiri, A., Gomez, A.: Echo from noise: synthetic ultrasound image generation using diffusion models for real image segmentation. In: International Workshop on Advances in Simplifying Medical Ultrasound, pp. 34–43. Springer (2023)
17. Wang, Z., Zhang, L., Wang, L., Zhang, Z.: Soft masked mamba diffusion model for CT to MRI conversion. arXiv preprint arXiv:2406.15910 (2024)
18. Wasserthal, J., et al.: Totalsegmentator: robust segmentation of 104 anatomic structures in CT images. Radiol. Artif. Intell. **5**(5), e230024 (2023)
19. Zhu, J.Y., Park, T., Isola, P., Efros, A.A.: Unpaired image-to-image translation using cycle-consistent adversarial networks. In: Proceedings of the IEEE International Conference on Computer Vision, pp. 2223–2232 (2017)

# Human-in-the-Loop Model Training

# Learning What is Worth Learning: Active and Sequential Domain Adaptation for Multi-modal Gross Tumor Volume Segmentation

Jingyun Yang, Guoqing Zhang, Jingge Wang, and Yang Li(✉)

Shenzhen Key Laboratory of Ubiquitous Data Enabling, Tsinghua Shenzhen International Graduate School, Tsinghua University, Beijing, China
yangli@sz.tsinghua.edu.cn

**Abstract.** Accurate gross tumor volume segmentation on multi-modal medical data is critical for radiotherapy planning in nasopharyngeal carcinoma and glioblastoma. Recent advances in deep neural networks have brought promising results in medical image segmentation, leading to an increasing demand for labeled data. Since labeling medical images is time-consuming and labor-intensive, active learning has emerged as a solution to reduce annotation costs by selecting the most informative samples to label and adapting high-performance models with as few labeled samples as possible. Previous active domain adaptation (ADA) methods seek to minimize sample redundancy by selecting samples that are farthest from the source domain. However, such one-off selection can easily cause negative transfer, and access to source medical data is often limited. Moreover, the query strategy for multi-modal medical data remains unexplored. In this work, we propose an active and sequential domain adaptation framework for dynamic multi-modal sample selection in ADA. We derive a query strategy to prioritize labeling and training on the most valuable samples based on their informativeness and representativeness. Empirical validation on diverse gross tumor volume segmentation tasks demonstrates that our method achieves favorable segmentation performance, significantly outperforming state-of-the-art ADA methods. Code is available at the git repository: mmActS.

**Keywords:** Gross tumor volume segmentation · Active domain adaptation · Sequential selection · Multi-modal learning

## 1 Introduction

Precise delineation of the Gross Tumor Volume (GTV) plays a pivotal role in ensuring effective radiotherapy for prevalent malignancies such as nasopharyngeal carcinoma, predominantly impacting the head and neck area [21], and glioblastoma, presumably originating from glial cells and posing a severe threat

---

J. Yang, G. Zhang—contributed equally to this work.

to human health [14]. Magnetic Resonance Imaging (MRI) is widely used for tumor detection due to its high soft tissue contrast and non-invasive nature, while multi-modal MRI data can map various tumor-induced tissue changes [23]. For example, FLAIR highlights tissue water relaxation differences, while post-Gadolinium T1 reveals intratumoral contrast uptake [1].

Manual GTV delineation on multi-modal MRI images is time-consuming and subject to inter-observer variability. Recent advances in deep learning have brought promising results in automatic medical image analysis, yielding successful models for various segmentation tasks [4,13,24]. However, the generalization capability of these models is limited by the large variability in training data and the lack of labeled data.

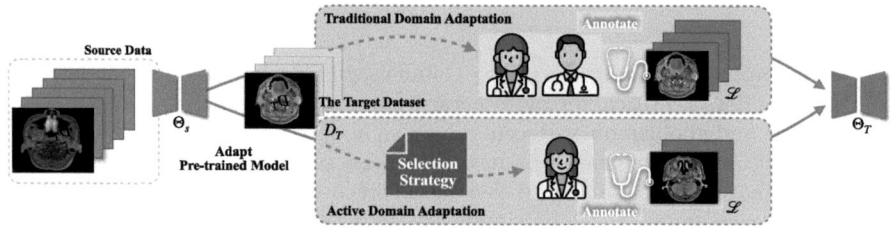

**Fig. 1.** Active domain adaptation aims to adapt models pre-trained on adequate source data, which is usually not accessible in medical scenarios, for the desired target task with as few labeled samples as possible.

One approach to ensuring reliable and robust model adaptation is Active Domain Adaptation (ADA) [20], where the most informative samples are actively selected to be labeled and fine-tune high-performance models with as few labeled samples as possible, as shown in Fig. 1. Previous ADA methods seek to minimize the sample redundancy either by optimizing for minimal cosine similarity to existing training data [11], or by combining source feature embeddings as the clustering reference [21]. However, these approaches presuppose access to source data—an assumption that often fails in medical imaging due to regulatory constraints and ethical concerns. Source-free methods [18,20] try to select samples with higher epistemic uncertainty based on prediction probabilities with a single forward pass. Nonetheless, such static one-off selection schemes, which neglect the evolving training dynamics and the inherent domain shift, can easily cause negative transfer. Moreover, none of the aforementioned methods fully explore the characteristics of multi-modal medical images, e.g., multi-sequence MRI. Works like [6] utilize transformer layers to integrate features extracted from each modality, while self-attention-based convolution methods enable weighted fusion of multi-modal MRI data [10]. This raises the question: how can multi-modal data be actively combined to better adapt the model?

To address the above issues, we propose an active and sequential domain adaptation framework for advancing gross tumor volume segmentation on multi-modal data in a source-free manner. To the best of our knowledge, this is the first work to propose a query strategy for multi-modal medical data. Using a novel dynamic sample selection strategy, we prioritize labeling and training on samples that are worth learning. Specifically, in each selection round, we estimate the uncertainty, objective abundance, and density of each sample as indicators of their informativeness and representativeness. Taking into account all these factors, we identify the most valuable sample in the current state. Then, a dominant modality election procedure is introduced to select the modality that exhibits promising performance for annotation, substantially reducing the annotation burden. By optimizing the use of rare medical resources, both multi-modal data and clinician efforts, our method significantly enhances GTV segmentation. Extensive experiments on benchmark 3D MRI datasets with various tumor segmentation tasks validate the effectiveness of our method, outperforming all the other state-of-the-art ADA methods. We believe our proposed approach will better leverage rare medical resources, including multi-modal data and clinician expertise, to adapt a model for the desired target task in a fast and scalable way. In summary, our main contributions are:

- **An active and sequential domain adaptation framework**: we propose a novel framework that dynamically selects the most valuable samples to learn, enabling an effective adaptation of well-trained source models to target tasks in a source-free manner with as few labeled samples as possible.
- **An multi-modal sample query strategy**: we derive an effective query strategy for dynamic multi-modal sample selection and significantly reduce labeling costs, optimizing the use of rare medical resources.

## 2 Methodology

In this section, we present the proposed active and sequential domain adaptation framework in the context of multi-modal medical image segmentation, shown in Fig. 2. First, we clarify the setting of active learning with multi-modal data. Then we introduce the sequential query strategy and define the selection criterion, with the consideration of the informativeness and representativeness of each sample. Finally, we describe the target model fine-tuning procedure.

### 2.1 Problem Definition

**ADA problem setting.** For active learning problems, given a target domain dataset $\mathcal{D}_\mathcal{T} = \{\mathbf{x}_i\}_{i=1}^n$, we select the most valuable samples to label and learn. Assuming access to a source model $\Theta_s$, pre-trained on adequate source domain data that is not always accessible in medical scenarios, the goal is to adapt $\Theta_s$ to achieve high performance on $\mathcal{D}_\mathcal{T}$ with as few labeled samples as possible.

**Multi-modal Learning.** Let us represent the M-modality sample with $\mathbf{x}_i = \{m_i^{(l)}\}_{l=1}^M$ where $m_i^{(l)}$ is the $l$-th modality scan of sample $\mathbf{x}_i$. To effectively fuse information from multiple modalities, we train the model in a multi-channel

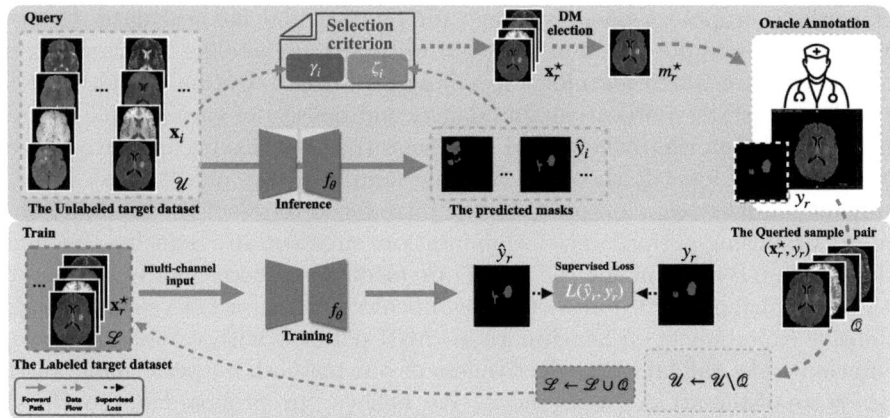

**Fig. 2.** Illustration of our active and sequential domain adaptation framework. The blue block shows the $r$-th query round while the pink block represents the target model's fine-tuning under the supervision of the updated labeled set $\mathcal{L}$.(Color figure online)

manner. Specifically, we stack the different modalities along the channel dimension, forming a multi-channel input fed into the model. The convolutional layers process all channels jointly, enabling the model to capture both modality-specific and cross-modality features for improved representation learning.

### 2.2 Query Strategy

Instead of a one-off selection, we sequentially select the most valuable samples until the labeling budget $\mathcal{B}$ is exhausted, as the model evolves and the most informative sample changes at each time step. We derive a selection criterion to assess each sample in the unlabeled pool $\mathcal{U} \subseteq \mathcal{D}_\mathcal{T}$. In the $r$-th selection round, the most valuable sample $x_r^*$ is selected and future undergoes a dominant modality (DM) election procedure for all $m_r^{(l)} \in \mathbf{x}_r^*$ to identify the modality $l^*$ that exhibits more promising performance than others. Next we query the label for scan $m_r^\star$ from oracle, yielding the labeled pair $(\mathbf{x}_r^\star, y_r)$. Then the model is trained on the labeled set $\mathcal{L} = \{(\mathbf{x}_1^\star, y_1), ..., (\mathbf{x}_r^\star, y_r)\}$ from this selection round to the next.

**Selection criterion.** In domain adaptation tasks, the source model $\Theta_\mathcal{S}$ has already acquired some fundamental knowledge [7].

To achieve good target performance, we estimate the informativeness and representativeness of each sample to capture the complexities and variabilities in the target data. Given a labeling budget, we prioritize annotating and training on samples that are worth learning, enabling the model to learn robust representation capabilities.

At the time step $t$, we have the current model $f_{\theta_t}$ and obtain the predicted mask $\hat{y}_i$ for sample $\mathbf{x}_i$: $\hat{y}_i = \arg\max_c(\text{softmax}_c(f_{\theta_t}(\mathbf{x}_i)))$.

**Algorithm 1.** Active and sequential fine-tuning with Multi-modal data.

**Require:** $\mathcal{D}_\mathcal{T} = \{\mathbf{x}_i\}_{i=1}^n$: The target dataset
**Require:** $f_\theta$: Parameterized model
**Require:** $\mathcal{B}, \tau$: Labeling budget, query stride
1: **Initialize:** $f_{\theta_0} = \Theta_s$ ; $\mathcal{U} \leftarrow \{x_i\}_{i=1}^n$ ; $\mathcal{L} \leftarrow \varnothing$ ; selection round $r = 1$
2: **for** $t = 0, 1, \ldots, T$ **do**
3:     **if** $r \leq \mathcal{B} \wedge t = \frac{r(r-1)}{2}\tau$ **then**
4:         Compute $s(\mathbf{x}), \forall \mathbf{x} \in \mathcal{U}$ according to Equation.6
5:         Select the most valuable sample $\mathbf{x}_r^* = \arg\max_{\mathbf{x} \in \mathcal{U}} s(\mathbf{x})$
6:         Identify the dominant modality scan $m_r^*$ according to Equation.7
7:         Query the label $y_r$ for $m_r^*$ from oracle, yielding $\mathcal{Q} = (\mathbf{x}_r^*, y_r)$, $r \leftarrow r + 1$
8:         Update the labeled and unlabeled sets $\mathcal{L} \leftarrow \mathcal{L} \cup \mathcal{Q}$ ; $\mathcal{U} \leftarrow \mathcal{U} \setminus \mathcal{Q}$
9:     **end if**
10:   **end if**
11:     Update model parameters w.r.t. $\mathcal{L}$
12: **end for**
13: **end for**
14: **return** $f_\theta$

In the $r$-th selection round, we quantify the informativeness $\zeta_i$ of sample $\mathbf{x}_i$, by jointly considering its predictive uncertainty $\mu_i$ and the objective abundance, estimated via the total predicted volume:

$$\zeta_i = \mu_i \sum\nolimits_{v_k \in \hat{y}_i} \mathbf{1}(v_k = 1), \tag{1}$$

where the summation $\sum_{v_k \in \hat{y}_i}$ denotes the number of voxels predicted as foreground in the segmentation mask $\hat{y}_i$. The uncertainty score $\mu_i$ is computed as the mean voxel-wise entropy across all predictions for sample $\mathbf{x}_i$. Specifically, for a model output $f_{\theta_t}$ with $C$ classes and $K$ voxels, we define:

$$\mu_i = \frac{1}{K} \sum_{u_k \in U_i} U_i = \frac{1}{K} \sum_{u_k \in U_i} \sum_{c=1}^{C} \mathcal{H}(\text{softmax}_c(f_{\theta_t}(\mathbf{x}_i)))), \tag{2}$$

where $\mathcal{H}(.)$ denotes the entropy function and $U_i$ is the voxel-level uncertainty map. Inspired by [22], two components in the measure are interpreted as follows: 1) *uncertainty* cue, and 2) *concentration* cue. The former identifies data that the model cannot predict confidently, while the latter indicates data with a higher concentration of objectives, necessitating oracle annotation for precise model training and refinement.

Meanwhile, we quantify the representativeness of $\mathbf{x}_i$ based on its density,

$$\gamma_i = \sum\nolimits_{\mathbf{x}_j \in \mathcal{U}, j \neq i} e^{-\left(\frac{\omega(\mathbf{x}_i, \mathbf{x}_j)}{\omega_d}\right)^2}, \tag{3}$$

where $\omega(\mathbf{x}_i, \mathbf{x}_j)$ is the distance between samples $\mathbf{x}_i$ and $\mathbf{x}_j$ measured by the Wasserstein distance [16] for its ability to handle shifts in data distributions and

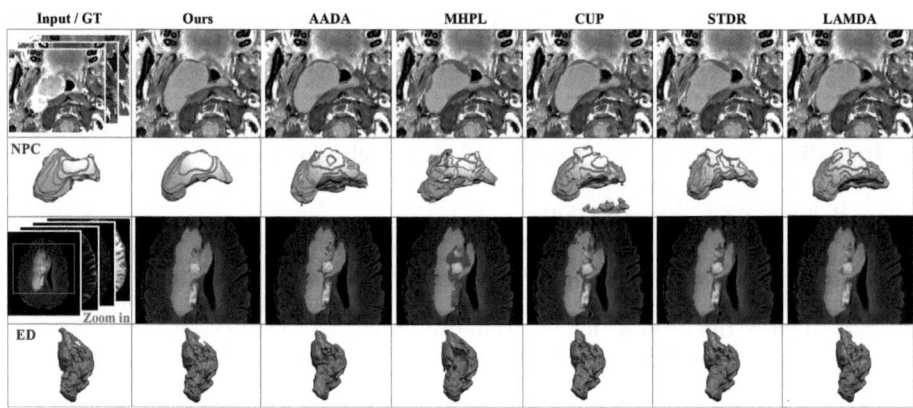

**Fig. 3.** Visualization of SOTA active domain adaptation methods performance. In the first and third rows, the pixels of 2D slices highlighted in red represent *incorrect predictions*, while the second and fourth rows offer 3D comparisons. (Color figure online)

$\omega_d$ is the neighborhood distance threshold. Specifically, given a pair of samples $(\mathbf{x}_i, \mathbf{x}_j)$ with M modalities, $\omega(\mathbf{x}_i, \mathbf{x}_j)$ is defined as:

$$\omega(\mathbf{x}_i, \mathbf{x}_j) \triangleq \frac{1}{M} \sum_{l=1}^{M} \mathcal{W}(\hat{P}_i^{(l)}, \hat{P}_j^{(l)}), \tag{4}$$

where $(\hat{P}_i^{(l)}, \hat{P}_j^{(l)})$ are distributions of images $(\hat{m}_i^{(l)}, \hat{m}_j^{(l)})$ after dimension reduction using principal components analysis. And the data-pair Wasserstein distance is defined as:

$$\mathcal{W}(\hat{P}_i^{(l)}, \hat{P}_j^{(l)}) = \inf_{\gamma \in \Pi\left(\hat{P}_i^{(l)}, \hat{P}_j^{(l)}\right)} \mathbb{E}_{(x,y) \sim \gamma} \|x - y\|. \tag{5}$$

Finally, the selection criterion $s(\mathbf{x}_i)$ for unlabeled target data is written as:

$$s(\mathbf{x}_i) = \zeta_i \gamma_i. \tag{6}$$

Accordingly, in the $r$-th selection round, the most valuable sample $\mathbf{x}_r^\star$ is selected, $\mathbf{x}_r^\star = \arg\max_{\mathbf{x}_i \in \mathcal{U}} s(\mathbf{x}_i)$, and future undergoes a DM election procedure to identify the dominant modality scan for annotation.

**Label Query.** In the dominant modality election procedure, a validation process is applied: For the selected sample $\mathbf{x}_r^\star$, the modality that exhibits promising performance is selected to be annotated. Formally, we have:

$$m_r^\star = \arg\max_{l \in \{1,\ldots,M\}} d(f_{\theta_t}(m_r^{(l)}), \hat{y}_r), \tag{7}$$

where the pseudo-label $\hat{y}_r$ is estimated by $f_{\theta_t}(\mathbf{x}_r^\star)$, $l$ indexes different modalities, $f_{\theta_t}$ is the current model, and $d(.,.)$ is the function to calculate the dice score. We query the label for the dominant modality scan $m_r^\star$ from oracle (e.g., doctors), yielding the labeled pair $\mathcal{Q} = (\mathbf{x}_r^\star, y_r)$ and the updated labeled set $\mathcal{L} \leftarrow \mathcal{L} \cup \mathcal{Q}$.

## 2.3 Active and Sequential Model Training

After the $r$-th oracle annotation round, we train the model using the labeled set $\mathcal{L} = \{(\mathbf{x}_1^\star, y_1), ..., (\mathbf{x}_r^\star, y_r)\}$ in a supervised manner. It is worth noting that if the model initialization is not proper to start the active learning process, it may produce meaningless informativeness estimation for the target domain [20]. A one-off selection based on such criteria can easily cause negative transfer. To mitigate this, we sequentially select the most valuable sample to label in each query round, based on the model's current state, until the labeling budget is reached, i.e., $r = \mathcal{B}$, and fine-tune the model incrementally. After the final query round, the labeled samples remain significantly fewer than the total target samples. i.e., $|\mathcal{L}| = \mathcal{B} \ll \mathcal{D}_\mathcal{T}$. As the extra computational cost for sample assessment is minimal (on the order of seconds), the query strategy adds negligible overhead. The proposed algorithm is shown in Algorithm 1.

**Table 1.** Results of active domain adaptation strategies on GTV segmentation 3D MRI datasets BraTS 2022 (ET, NCR, ED) and NPC 2024. $|\mathcal{L}|$: the number of labeled target samples. Bold number: best score except for the upper bound.

| Method | | ET | | NCR | | ED | | NPC | |
|---|---|---|---|---|---|---|---|---|---|
| Strategy | $|\mathcal{L}|$ | Dice (%) | mIoU (%) | Dice (%) | mIoU (%) | Dice (%) | mIoU (%) | Dice (%) | mIoU (%) |
| Lower bound | 0 | 77.70 | 64.39 | 61.51 | 49.46 | 69.85 | 56.15 | 67.63 | 51.71 |
| Upper bound | 80 | 94.10 | 89.20 | 78.94 | 69.72 | 92.25 | 87.37 | 76.12 | 61.85 |
| Random Selection | 3 | 78.09 | 67.52 | 60.12 | 51.72 | 73.33 | 59.73 | 66.51 | 51.07 |
| AADA (WACV' 20) | 3 | 81.51 | 74.53 | 65.66 | 56.95 | 76.30 | 64.20 | 69.71 | 53.91 |
| MHPL (CVPR' 23) | 3 | 88.63 | 79.62 | 62.85 | 51.72 | 77.67 | 68.32 | 68.01 | 52.81 |
| CUP (MICCAI' 24) | 3 | 83.60 | 75.12 | 64.68 | 47.80 | 77.58 | 67.74 | 69.04 | 53.79 |
| STDR (TMI' 24) | 3 | 88.65 | 81.09 | 62.53 | 50.86 | 78.08 | 68.84 | 71.96 | 56.95 |
| LAMDA (ECCV'22) | 3 | 89.45 | 80.91 | 66.50 | 49.81 | 78.67 | 68.74 | 71.17 | 56.26 |
| Ours | 3 | **91.11** | **84.13** | **72.30** | **64.14** | **82.82** | **74.10** | **74.69** | **59.96** |

## 3 Experiments and Results

### 3.1 Datasets and Training Setup

Two multi-modal GTV segmentation datasets are used in our work: BraTS 2022 [2,3,14] and NPC 2024 [12,21]. BraTS 2022 includes 3D MRI volumes across FLAIR, T1, T1c, and T2 modalities, segmenting for enhancing tumor (ET), edema (ED), and necrotic core (NCR). NPC 2024 is characterized by nasopharyngeal carcinoma (NPC) and manually delineated on each slice of the patient's T1, T1c, and T2 MRI images. For both datasets, we use 80 cases for training and 20 for evaluation. We implement all methods on pre-trained nnU-Net [9] for all experiments, following the pre-training settings of MONAI [4]. The models are trained using an A800 80GB GPU for a maximum of 600 epochs with a batch size of 5 and an initial learning rate of 0.01, decayed following the poly learning rate policy [5]. For the query strategy, the selection stride is set to 40 epochs. For the label budget, following the common few-shot active learning setting in [15], all the experiments are conducted under a 1-way 3-shot scenario using 5-fold cross-validation. We experimented with budgets of labeling 5, 3, 2, and 1 target samples, and found that using 3 samples strikes a good balance, achieving satisfactory performance while keeping annotation costs low.

### 3.2 Performance evaluation

**Table 2.** Ablation study on single- and multi-modal learning in our method.

| Modality | ET | | NCR | | ED | | NPC | |
|---|---|---|---|---|---|---|---|---|
| | Dice (%) | mIoU (%) | Dice (%) | mIoU (%) | Dice (%) | mIoU (%) | Dice (%) | mIoU (%) |
| FLAIR | 46.06 | 31.62 | 37.75 | 26.77 | 73.21 | 59.99 | - | - |
| T1 | 13.96 | 8.84 | 35.01 | 25.69 | 51.09 | 38.27 | 64.47 | 50.18 |
| T1c | 87.26 | 79.30 | 64.59 | 55.85 | 59.63 | 47.97 | 69.36 | 53.67 |
| T2 | 22.87 | 14.57 | 39.91 | 28.99 | 63.47 | 51.30 | 66.11 | 51.71 |
| Multiple | **91.11** | **84.13** | **72.30** | **64.14** | **82.82** | **74.10** | **74.69** | **59.96** |

To investigate the effectiveness and efficiency of ADA, we consider two baselines: direct inference without fine-tuning (lower bound) and fine-tuning the model with all samples labeled (upper bound). Meanwhile, we compare our framework with five state-of-the-art ADA methods, alongside random selection: 1) AADA [17] adversarially adapts the model with importance sampling, 2) MHPL [19] exploits minimum happy points based on neighbor uncertainty and diversity, 3) STDR [21] selects domain-invariant and -specific samples referenced to source domain points, 4) a cascade sampling strategy CUP [22] based on prediction informativeness, 5) a multi-round selection strategy LAMDA [8] with label distribution matching using a density-aware active sampling. We keep the label ratio and query stride the same, ensuring a consistent analysis. We evaluate the segmentation performance using the Dice score and the mean IoU. A quantitative analysis of model adaptation performance on BraTS 2022 and NPC 2024 datasets is detailed in Table. 1 and visualized in Fig. 3. The results are averaged over three independent runs with different training data splits to ensure robustness. Our proposed framework significantly outperforms all state-of-the-art ADA methods on both datasets across anatomical regions. Compared to random selection, it achieves an average Dice score gain of **16.62%** on BraTS 2022 and **12.23%** on NPC 2024. Furthermore, compared to LAMDA, our method yields an average Dice gain of **5.28%** on BraTS 2022 and **4.95%** on NPC 2024.

**Effectiveness of Sequential Selection.** Adequate source data for label matching and joint training is usually not available in medical scenes. To further investigate the effectiveness of sequential selection, we conducted one-off selection experiments. For the NPC 2024 dataset, one-off selection with our criterion achieves a Dice score of 0.7103, compared to 0.7117 with LAMDA, 0.7196 with STDR, and **0.7469** with our sequential selection. For the BraTS 2022 dataset, our one-off selection yields an average Dice score of 0.8072, outperforming LAMDA (0.7821) and STDR (0.7642), while our sequential selection achieves the highest score of **0.8208**. These results highlight the superiority of our sequential selection scheme without relying on any source domain data while achieving SOTA performance.

**Effectiveness of Multi-modal Learning.** The results in Table. 2 show that multi-modal learning can indeed enhance tumor segmentation. Clinicians often provide scans with multiple modalities since multi-sequence data is easily collected, making it more efficient to use all available data rather than randomly choosing a single modality, especially given the performance variations observed in ET results.

## 4 Conclusion and Future Work

We propose a novel source-free active and sequential domain adaptation framework for advancing GTV segmentation on multi-modal medical data. Experiments on two benchmark medical datasets demonstrate that the proposed method achieves state-of-the-art performance in ADA problems within the realm of medical image processing. One limitation of our method lies in the informativeness criterion that is adapted from [22], originally proposed for vessel segmentation tasks. While it effectively identifies salient regions, it tends to bias the selection toward larger tumors. This can be problematic in datasets with varying tumor sizes, leading to suboptimal performance on early-stage or small-sized tumors. Moreover, our current experiments are limited to U-Net-based architectures. For future research, we plan to incorporate more advanced foundation models such as Med-SAM[13] and explore robust sampling strategies to improve segmentation performance on small but significant lesions and enhance the overall clinical utility of our approach.

**Acknowledgments.** This work is supported in part by the Natural Science Foundation of China (Grant 62371270).

**Disclosure of Interests.** The authors have no conflicts of interest to declare that are relevant to the content of this article.

# References

1. Bai, J.W., Qiu, S.Q., Zhang, G.J.: Molecular and functional imaging in cancer-targeted therapy: current applications and future directions. Signal Transduct. Target. Ther. **8**(1), 89 (2023)

2. Baid, U., et al.: The RSNA-ASNR-MICCAI brats 2021 benchmark on brain tumor segmentation and radiogenomic classification. arXiv preprint arXiv:2107.02314 (2021)
3. Bakas, S., et al.: Advancing the cancer genome atlas glioma MRI collections with expert segmentation labels and radiomic features. Sci. Data **4**(1), 1–13 (2017)
4. Cardoso, M.J., et al.: MONAI: an open-source framework for deep learning in healthcare. arXiv preprint arXiv:2211.02701 (2022)
5. Chen, L.C., Papandreou, G., Kokkinos, I., Murphy, K., Yuille, A.L.: DeepLab: semantic image segmentation with deep convolutional nets, atrous convolution, and fully connected CRFS. IEEE Trans. Pattern Anal. Mach. Intell. **40**(4), 834–848 (2017)
6. Cho, J., Park, J.: Hybrid-fusion transformer for multisequence MRI. In: International Conference on Medical Imaging and Computer-Aided Diagnosis, pp. 477–487. Springer (2022)
7. Guan, H., Liu, M.: Domain adaptation for medical image analysis: a survey. IEEE Trans. Biomed. Eng. **69**(3), 1173–1185 (2021)
8. Hwang, S., Lee, S., Kim, S., Ok, J., Kwak, S.: Combating label distribution shift for active domain adaptation. In: European Conference on Computer Vision, pp. 549–566. Springer (2022). https://doi.org/10.1007/978-3-031-19827-4_32
9. Isensee, F., Jaeger, P.F., Kohl, S.A., Petersen, J., Maier-Hein, K.H.: NNU-Net: a self-configuring method for deep learning-based biomedical image segmentation. Nat. Methods **18**(2), 203–211 (2021)
10. Jia, X., Liu, Y., Yang, Z., Yang, D.: Multi-modality self-attention aware deep network for 3D biomedical segmentation. BMC Med. Inform. Decis. Mak. **20**, 1–7 (2020)
11. Li, G., et al.: Hybrid representation-enhanced sampling for Bayesian active learning in musculoskeletal segmentation of lower extremities. Int. J. Comput. Assist. Radiol. Surg., 1–10 (2024). https://doi.org/10.1007/s11548-024-03065-7
12. Luo, X., et al.: Deep learning-based accurate delineation of primary gross tumor volume of nasopharyngeal carcinoma on heterogeneous magnetic resonance imaging: A large-scale and multi-center study. Radiother. Oncol. **180**, 109480 (2023)
13. Ma, J., He, Y., Li, F., Han, L., You, C., Wang, B.: Segment anything in medical images. Nat. Commun. **15**(1), 654 (2024)
14. Menze, B.H., et al.: The multimodal brain tumor image segmentation benchmark (brats). IEEE Trans. Med. Imaging **34**(10), 1993–2024 (2014)
15. Ouyang, C., Biffi, C., Chen, C., Kart, T., Qiu, H., Rueckert, D.: Self-supervised learning for few-shot medical image segmentation. IEEE Trans. Med. Imaging **41**(7), 1837–1848 (2022)
16. Panaretos, V.M., Zemel, Y.: Statistical aspects of Wasserstein distances. Ann. Rev. Stat. Appl. **6**, 405–431 (2019)
17. Su, J.C., Tsai, Y.H., Sohn, K., Liu, B., Maji, S., Chandraker, M.: Active adversarial domain adaptation. In: Proceedings of the IEEE/CVF Winter Conference on Applications of Computer Vision, pp. 739–748 (2020)
18. Tang, Y., et al.: PLD-AL: pseudo-label divergence-based active learning in carotid intima-media segmentation for ultrasound images. In: International Conference on Medical Image Computing and Computer-Assisted Intervention, pp. 57–67. Springer (2023). https://doi.org/10.1007/978-3-031-43895-0_6
19. Wang, F., Han, Z., Zhang, Z., He, R., Yin, Y.: MHPL: minimum happy points learning for active source free domain adaptation. In: Proceedings of the IEEE/CVF Conference on Computer Vision and Pattern Recognition, pp. 20008–20018 (2023)

20. Wang, H., Jin, Q., Li, S., Liu, S., Wang, M., Song, Z.: A comprehensive survey on deep active learning in medical image analysis. Med. Image Anal. **95**, 103201 (2024)
21. Wang, H., et al.: Dual-reference source-free active domain adaptation for nasopharyngeal carcinoma tumor segmentation across multiple hospitals. IEEE Trans. Med. Imaging **43**(12), 4078–4090 (2024)
22. Wang, H., et al.: Advancing UWF-SLO vessel segmentation with source-free active domain adaptation and a novel multi-center dataset. In: Linguraru, M.G., et al. (eds.) International Conference on Medical Image Computing and Computer-Assisted Intervention, pp. 75–85. Springer (2024). https://doi.org/10.1007/978-3-031-72114-4_8
23. Wang, H., Ma, C., Zhang, J., Zhang, Y., Avery, J., Hull, L., Carneiro, G.: Learnable cross-modal knowledge distillation for multi-modal learning with missing modality. In: Greenspan, H., et al. (eds.) International Conference on Medical Image Computing and Computer-Assisted Intervention, pp. 216–226. Springer (2023). https://doi.org/10.1007/978-3-031-43901-8_21
24. Wang, Z., Zheng, J.Q., Zhang, Y., Cui, G., Li, L.: Mamba-UNet: UNet-like pure visual mamba for medical image segmentation. arXiv preprint arXiv:2402.05079 (2024)

# Guided Active Learning for Medical Image Segmentation

Bernhard Föllmer[1,2](✉)[iD], Vladimir Serafimoski[1], Kenrick Schulze[1][iD], Federico Biavati[1][iD], Sebastian Stober[3][iD], Wojciech Samek[4,5,6][iD], and Marc Dewey[1,7,8][iD]

[1] Department of Radiology, Charité-Universitätsmedizin Berlin, corporate member of Freie Universität Berlin and Humboldt-Universität zu Berlin, 10117 Berlin, Germany
[2] Inria, Epione Team, Sophia Antipolis, Université Côte d'Azur, Nice, France
bernhard.foellmer@charite.de
[3] Artificial Intelligence Lab, Otto-von-Guericke-Universität, Magdeburg, Germany
[4] Department of Artificial Intelligence, Fraunhofer Heinrich Hertz Institute, Berlin, Germany
[5] BIFOLD Berlin Institute for the Foundations of Learning and Data, Berlin, Germany
[6] Department of Electrical Engineering and Computer Science, Technical University of Berlin, Berlin, Germany
[7] DZHK (German Centre for Cardiovascular Research), partner site Berlin, Germany
[8] Deutsches Herzzentrum der Charité (DHZC), Berlin, Germany

**Abstract.** Active learning has the potential to reduce labeling costs in medical image segmentation by selecting only the most informative samples. However, conventional approaches typically rely on model-based informativeness measures, limiting the expert's role to passively annotating pre-selected images. This restricts expert-driven prioritization of segmentation targets aligned with clinical objectives. To address this limitation, we propose **GALMIS** (**G**uided **A**ctive **L**earning for **M**edical **I**mage **S**egmentation), a novel framework that integrates expert-driven guidance into the informative sample selection process. By leveraging submodular subset selection, GALMIS ensures that selected samples are not only informative but also clinically relevant to predefined segmentation targets. We evaluate our approach in both *simulated* and *real* active learning scenarios on: (1) foreground-foreground class imbalance in abdominal CT, and (2) clinical targets for coronary artery segmentation in cardiac CT. Our results demonstrate improved labeling efficiency on clinically relevant targets compared to conventional active learning methods. Code is available at https://github.com/Berni1557/TAL.

**Keywords:** Targeted Active Learning · Human-in-the-Loop · Medical Image Segmentation · Submodular Subset Selection · Active Learning

## 1 Introduction

Medical image segmentation requires extensive voxel-wise annotations, a labor-intensive and time-consuming task typically performed by domain experts [2]. Active learning (AL) has emerged as a promising approach to alleviate this burden by iteratively selecting the most informative samples from an unlabeled dataset for expert annotation [23], primarily relying on informativeness measures such as uncertainty and diversity. However, a major limitation of conventional AL approaches in medical image segmentation is the *passive role* assigned to domain expert (annotator), who is restricted to manually annotate or correct selected samples. This overlooks an essential aspect of medical segmentation: its ultimate goal is not merely segmentation accuracy but rather supporting clinical decision making. Standard AL strategies fail to account for critical domain-specific challenges, such as:

1. **Foreground-foreground class imbalance:** A dataset imbalance problem where both over-represented and under-represented classes belong to the foreground, such as small or rare structures like pathological regions, making their segmentation particularly challenging [11].
2. **Annotation Uncertainty Differences Across Classes:** This problem occurs when multi-class annotations contain "strong" labels for certain classes while others have "weak" labels and can reduce the effectiveness of uncertainty-based active learning strategies.
3. **Expert-driven prioritization of segmentation targets:** Segmentation performance is particularly critical in specific cases or regions for clinical decision-making such as high risk anatomical structures.

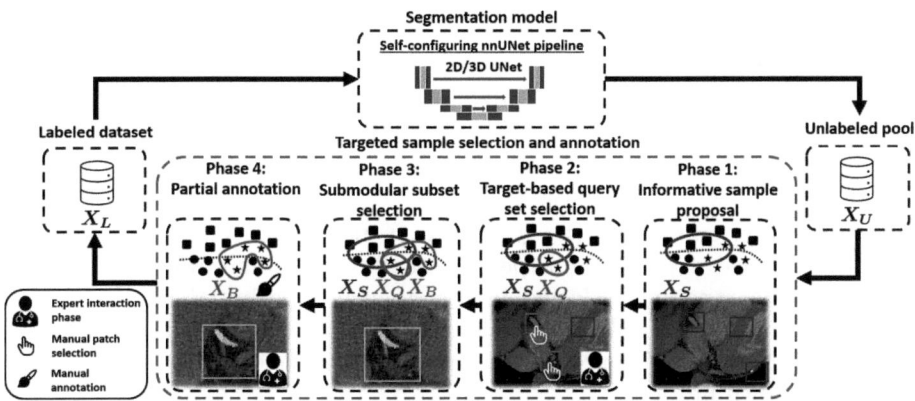

**Fig. 1.** Guided active learning pipeline. In each iteration, a model is trained on the labeled dataset and a four phase guided sample selection process is performed. This process is iteratively repeated over multiple rounds, progressively improving model performance for pre-defined segmentation target.

Targeted Active Learning (TAL) extends traditional AL by integrating domain-specific knowledge and predefined objectives into the learning process. TAL enables active expert participation, allowing experts to guide the model toward clinically relevant targets in each iteration. In this work, we introduce GALMIS (**G**uided **A**ctive **L**earning for **M**edical **I**mage **S**egmentation), a novel framework that enables expert-driven guidance in active learning for medical image segmentation. GALMIS actively incorporates expert preferences into the sample selection process, ensuring that selected samples are informative (uncertain, diverse) and aligned with segmentation objectives (segmentation targets) to ensure clinical relevance.

## 2 Related Work

**Active Learning for Medical Image Segmentation:** Active learning sampling strategies can be broadly categorized into uncertainty-based methods, which estimate epistemic uncertainty using techniques such as Monte Carlo Dropout [12], Bayesian neural networks [8], or ensembles [3]; and representation-based methods, which aim to maximize sample diversity and representativeness within a batch [21]. Hybrid strategies aim to balance uncertainty-based selection with redundancy minimization and diversity maximization [1,7,18,24].

**Targeted Active Learning:** Targeted active learning is a task-driven extension of active learning, where the model selectively queries data samples for annotation according to predefined segmentation goals, aiming to optimize label efficiency and task-specific model performance. Few studies have investigated TAL for medical image classification, primarily addressing challenges such as rare class representation, redundancy, and out-of-distribution samples [6,15,16]. However, its potential in complex segmentation tasks remains underexplored.

## 3 Method

### 3.1 Guided Active Learning Pipeline

We consider a dataset $\boldsymbol{X} = \{\boldsymbol{x}_i\}_{i=1}^{|\boldsymbol{X}|}$ where $\boldsymbol{x}_i \in \mathbb{R}^{h \times w \times d}$ represent a 3D patch of a medical image with dimension $h \times w \times d$. Let $\boldsymbol{X_U} = \{\boldsymbol{x}_i\}_{i=1}^{|\boldsymbol{X_U}|} \subseteq \boldsymbol{X}$ be the unlabeled subset and $\boldsymbol{X_L} = \{\boldsymbol{x}_i, \boldsymbol{y}_i\}_{i=1}^{|\boldsymbol{X_L}|} \subseteq \boldsymbol{X}$ be the labeled subset of $\boldsymbol{X}$. For the initial labeled dataset, the expert manually selects and annotates samples (patches) from randomly selected images to train the initial model. In each iteration, a model is trained on $\boldsymbol{X_L}$ followed by an informative and representative (targeted) sample selection process of a batch $\boldsymbol{X_B}$ for annotation. The processing pipeline is shown in Fig. 1.

### 3.2 Informative and Representative Sample Selection

The sample selection process is performed in four phases: 1) Informative Sample Proposal, 2) Target-based Query Set Selection, 3) Submodular Subset Selection, 4) Partial Annotation [19].

**Phase 1: Informative Sample Proposal:** First, uncertainty is estimated for all samples in the unlabeled dataset using Monte Carlo Dropout [8]. Subsequently, a subset $\mathbf{X}_S \subseteq \mathbf{X}_U$ is selected by sampling from a probability distribution over $\mathbf{X}_U$, where the selection probability is proportional to the estimated uncertainty, weighted by the inverse number of annotated voxels.

**Phase 2: Target-Based Query Set Selection:** To construct a query set $\mathbf{X}_Q$, the pre-selected set $\mathbf{X}_S$ is presented to the expert along with pseudo-labels. Relevant samples are manually selected by the expert through manual interaction, clicking on image patches deemed important for the predefined target, using a custom-built extension integrated into 3D Slicer. Additionally, the expert may choose patches, as the initially proposed samples are not always useful, particularly in early training rounds.

**Phase 3: Submodular Subset Selection:** Submodular subset selection is a principled approach for identifying representative and diverse subsets from large datasets [10,14]. Submodular functions exhibit a diminishing returns property, which allows for efficient and near-optimal selection of data points under budget constraints. In GALMIS, we adopt a submodular mutual information (SMI) framework to select a batch of samples $\mathbf{X}_B \subseteq \mathbf{X}_U$ that are both relevant to the expert-defined query set $\mathbf{X}_Q$ and diverse among themselves. We use the LogDet Conditional Mutual Information (LogDetMI) criterion [10] to quantify the similarity between the candidate batch and the query set: $I_f(\mathbf{X}_B; \mathbf{X}_Q) = \log\det(\mathbf{S}_B) - \log\det(\mathbf{S}_B - \eta^2 \mathbf{S}_{B,Q} \mathbf{S}_Q^{-1} \mathbf{S}_{B,Q}^\top)$ where $\mathbf{S}_B$, $\mathbf{S}_Q$, and $\mathbf{S}_{B,Q}$ are similarity matrices computed within the selected batch, within the query set, and between batch and query set, respectively. The submodular function is leveraged to select a subset that maximizes the mutual information criterion defined as $\mathbf{X}_B \leftarrow \operatorname{argmax}_{\mathbf{X}_B \subseteq \mathbf{X}_U, |\mathbf{X}_B| \leq B} I_f(\mathbf{X}_B; \mathbf{X}_Q)$. As similarity matrices, previous works proposed cosine similarity or approximated pairwise influence (Fisher kernel) [14]. In this work, we adopt the Fisher kernel, which has previously demonstrated success in deep active learning for medical image segmentation, as shown in USIM [7]. This formulation encourages the selection of samples that are similar to those identified as clinically important by the expert (via the query set), while avoiding redundancy.

**Phase 4: Partial Annotation with Pseudo Label Correction:** To perform cost-efficient annotation, the expert annotates the selected batch $\mathbf{X}_B$ by correcting pseudo labels provided by the segmentation model of the previous active learning round. To account for image areas that can not be annotated due to image artifacts (e.g. motion and metal artifacts, severe noise), an additional "NON-DIAGNOSTIC" label is used. The image regions labeled as "NON-DIAGNOSTIC" are excluded from loss computation.

## 4 Experiments and Results

### 4.1 Datasets and Segmentation Targets

**LIVER-GLAND Dataset.** We created a custom dataset to simulate foreground-foreground class imbalance [11] from the BTCV dataset for abdomen segmentation [17]. Specifically, we combined annotations for the liver (a large organ) and the left adrenal gland (a small organ) into a single foreground class, while merging all other classes into the background. We defined two performance targets:

**Target 1:** In the first scenario, the annotator aimed to optimize the model for segmentation of the left adrenal gland (Dice score).

**Target 2:** In the second scenario, the annotator aimed to optimize the model for the Macro-Dice (average Dice across the left adrenal gland and liver) of the left adrenal gland and liver.

**CORONARY-ARTERY dataset.** An unlabeled training set for coronary artery segmentation was constructed by randomly selecting 250 contrast-enhanced cardiac CT (CTA) scans from the DISCHARGE [4] and CAD-Man [5] trials. Six scans were identified as non-diagnostic due to excessive noise but were retained to preserve dataset realism. Performance was evaluated on 19 labeled CTA scans from the CAD-Man trial using the clDice metric, a topology-preserving metric for tubular structure segmentation [22]. Annotations include 18 coronary artery segment classes based on SCCT guidelines [20], plus an additional class for non-diagnostic regions ("weak" annotations). We defined four segmentation targets:

**Target 1:** The annotator aimed to improve overall segmentation performance of the all coronary arteries (Micro-Dice).

**Target 2:** The annotator aimed to improve segmentation performance of the distal right coronary artery (RCA) branches including distal RCA (dRCA), right posterior descending artery (RPDA) and right posterior-lateral branch (RPLB).

**Target 3:** The annotator aimed to improve segmentation performance of the distal left anterior descending artery.

**Target 4:** The annotator aimed to correct falsely segmented proximal RCA side branches. These side branches are not included in the 18-segment SCCT model and require re-labeling as background. Examples are shown in Fig. 2.

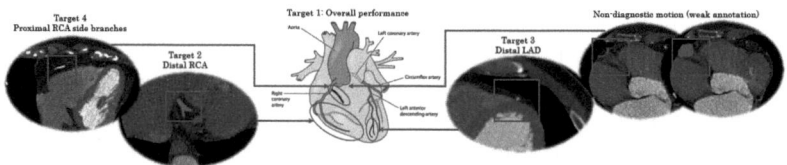

**Fig. 2.** Examples from the CORONARY-ARTERY dataset illustrating the four segmentation targets: Target 1 - Overall performance, Target 2 - Segmentation of distal RCA branches, Target 3 - Segmentation of distal LAD, Target 4 - Correction of incorrectly segmented proximal RCA branches and non-diagnostic annotation (weak annotation). 3D patches are highlighted with red rectangles. Image adapted from [13] (Color figure online).

**Experimental Details:** In our TAL pipeline, we used the self-configuring nnU-Net [9] to automatically generate overlapping 3D patches ($128 \times 128 \times 128$), select the optimal network architecture, and fine-tuned the model for 1000 epochs per round. For the LIVER-GLAND dataset, 7 queries were selected per round. Since the CORONARY-ARTERY dataset is more complex and searching for suitable query samples might be more time consuming, we did not set a fixed number of query samples but selected a 10-minute time limit for the selection of query samples. In both cases, query selection was performed manually by a domain expert. Batch sizes were 25 and 30 for the LIVER-GLAND and CORONARY-ARTERY datasets, respectively. Annotation was simulated for LIVER-GLAND, while manual annotation was performed for CORONARY-ARTERY using our in-house 3D Slicer extension. A 60-minute annotation time limit per round was applied across all methods. We compared our approach to Random Sampling (RANDOM), Mean STD [12] using Monte Carlo Dropout (MCD), BADGE [1], and USIM [7]. For BADGE, gradients were computed from the last convolutional layer, as commonly done in classification tasks. The parameter $\eta$, controlling the trade-off between target relevance and intra-batch diversity, was set to 1.0.

### 4.2 Guided Active Learning for Foreground-Foreground Class Imbalance Problem

To evaluate the effectiveness of our method for the foreground-foreground class imbalance problem, we used the LIVER-GLAD dataset. The model was trained under two scenarios, GALMIS - Target 1 and GALMIS - Target 2, to optimize for the two specific predefined segmentation targets.

**Quantitative and Qualitative Evaluation:** In Fig. 3 (A–C), GALMIS consistently outperforms competing methods on both segmentation targets: (1) the

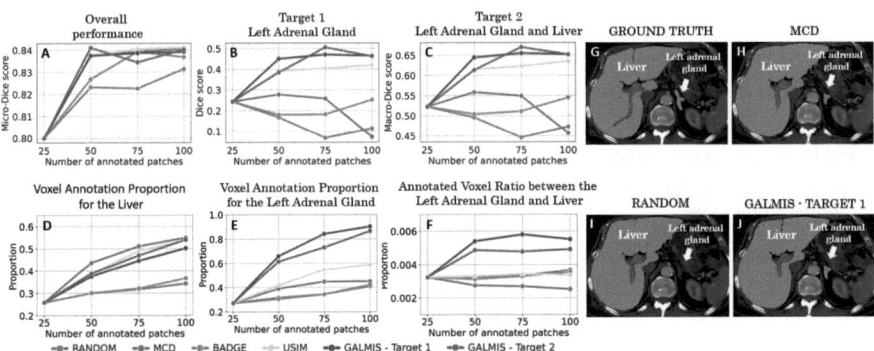

**Fig. 3.** Performance Comparison. (A) Overall segmentation performance assessed using the Micro-Dice score for the liver and left adrenal gland. (B) Segmentation performance of the left adrenal gland. (C) Macro-Dice score for the liver and adrenal gland. Proportion of annotated voxel of the left adrenal gland (D), liver (E) and ratio of annotated voxel from left adrenal gland and liver (F). Representative examples of ground truth segmentations and corresponding predictions from MCD, RANDOM, and GALMIS after the first TAL round are shown in panels GJ, respectively.

Dice score for the left adrenal gland and (2) the Macro-Dice score, demonstrating its effectiveness in addressing foreground–foreground class imbalance. Note that the Macro-Dice score is predominantly influenced by variations in the segmentation performance of the left adrenal gland. USIM also outperforms RANDOM, MCD, and BADGE, leveraging its integration of uncertainty, diversity, and representativity in the sampling strategy. We examined the proportion of annotated voxels and class imbalance between the left adrenal gland and liver (Fig. 3, D–F). The proportion of annotated liver voxels increases most rapidly for uncertainty-based methods, particularly MCD, followed by GALMIS–Target 2. In contrast, GALMIS shows faster growth in annotations for the left adrenal gland (Fig. 3E) and a steeper improvement in Macro-Dice (Fig. 3F), supporting its advantage in handling class imbalance where other methods struggle.

### 4.3 Guided Active Learning for Coronary Artery Segmentation

To evaluate GALMIS for segmentation tasks with different annotation uncertainty across classes and expert-driven prioritization of segmentation targets, we used the CORONARY-ARTERY dataset. We assessed the framework in four scenarios, each addressing a specific target introduced in Sect. 4.1.

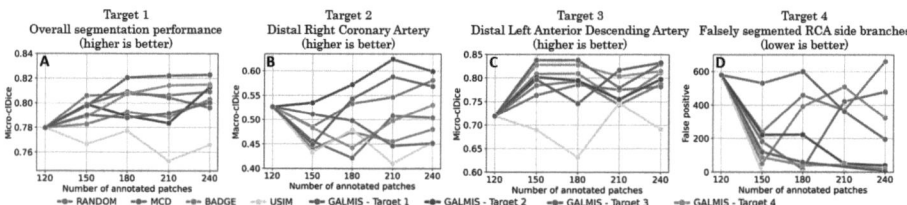

**Fig. 4.** Performance comparison between sampling strategies across four segmentation targets: (A) overall segmentation performance, (B) segmentation of distal RCA branches (dRCA, RPDA, RPLB), (C) segmentation of distal LAD, and (D) correction of misclassified proximal RCA branches.

**Quantitative and Qualitative Evaluation.** Performance development is shown in Fig. 4. GALMIS achieves strong target-specific results across all tasks, with GALMIS - Target 1, which jointly optimizes all targets, yielding the best overall performance. While the target-specific variants (Targets 2-4) perform well on their respective objectives, they show suboptimal overall performance due to their narrow focus. Interestingly, methods such as USIM, MCD, and BADGE exhibit a decline in performance as additional samples are acquired—an unexpected outcome. A possible explanation is provided in Fig. 5A, which illustrates that RANDOM often selects uninformative patches, while MCD and USIM tend to sample non-diagnostic regions driven by elevated uncertainty. In contrast, GALMIS consistently focuses on clinically relevant structures, such as the distal right coronary artery (RCA). This is further confirmed by the quantitative analysis in Fig. 5B, where MCD, BADGE, and USIM predominantly select patches from non-diagnostic scans, focusing on outliers and thereby limiting or even reducing performance. Finally, we analyzed how many selected patches contained annotations of the major coronary arteries (LAD, LCX, RCA) across all three training rounds (Fig. 5C). Notably, USIMFT selected more foreground-containing patches than MCD and USIM. Target-specific variants (USIMFTRCA, USIMFTSIDE, USIMTFLAD) also exhibited clear anatomical preferences, selecting more patches from their corresponding target arteries.

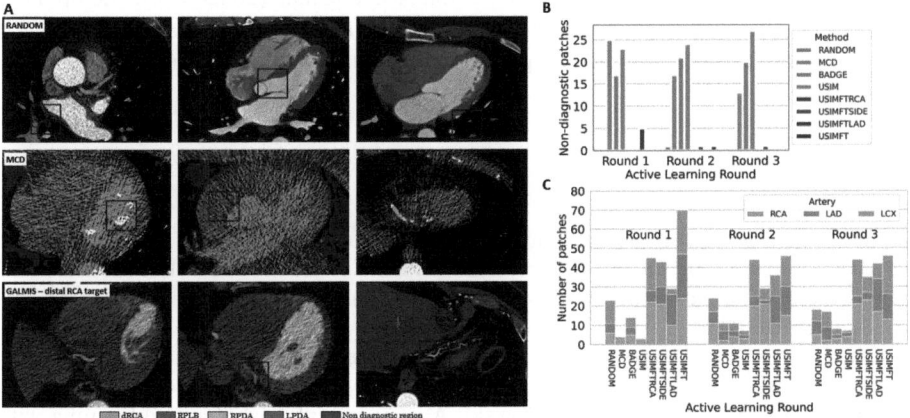

**Fig. 5.** Representative examples of selected batches for the distal RCA target using GALMIS, RANDOM, and MCD are shown in panel (A). Panel (B) displays the number of patches selected from non-diagnostic scans (outliers), while panel (C) shows the number of selected patches containing pseudo-labels of the main coronary arteries (LAD, LCX, and RCA). Note that patches containing multiple arteries are counted once for each corresponding artery.

## 5 Conclusion

In this study, we proposed GALMIS, a guided active learning framework for medical image segmentation. Our results demonstrate its effectiveness in improving both target-specific and overall segmentation performance. By integrating expert priorities, GALMIS enhances label efficiency in complex annotation scenarios. Its benefit may be limited, however, when no specific target is defined or when existing methods already capture the relevant regions. Further evaluation is needed to assess its utility for more complex, clinically aligned targets.

**Acknowledgments.** We thank Hervé Delingette for his insightful comments on this work.

**Disclosure of Interests.** W.S. was supported by the Federal Ministry of Education and Research (BMBF) as grant BIFOLD (01IS18025A, 01IS18037II) and the German Research Foundation (DFG) as research unit DeSBi KI-FOR 5363 (459422098).

M.D.: Grants: EU (EC-GA 603266 in HEALTH.2013.2.4.2-2) DFG (DE 1361/14-1, DE 1361/18-1/2, BIOQIC GRK 2260/1, Radiomics DE 1361/19-1 [428222922] and 20-1 [428223139] in SPP 2177/1), GUIDE-IT (DE 1361/24-1), Berlin University Alliance (GC_SC_PC 27), G-BA (01NVF23002), Berlin Institute of Health (Digital Health Accelerator). Editor: Cardiac CT (Springer Nature). Other: Hands-on cardiac CT courses (www.ct-kurs.de) Institutional research agreements: Siemens, General Electric, Philips, Canon. Patent on fractal analysis of perfusion imaging (jointly with Florian Michallek, EPO 2022 EP3350773A1, and USPTO 2021 10,991,109, approved) M.D. is European Society of Radiology (ESR) Publications Chair (2022-2025); the opinions expressed in this presentation are the author's own and do not represent the view of ESR. All other authors have no competing interests to declare that are relevant to the content of this article.

# References

1. Ash, J.T., Zhang, C., Krishnamurthy, A., Langford, J., Agarwal, A.: Deep batch active learning by diverse, uncertain gradient lower bounds. In: International Conference on Learning Representations (2020). https://openreview.net/forum?id=ryghZJBKPS
2. Chen, C., et al.: Deep learning for cardiac image segmentation: a review. Front. Cardiov. Med. **7** (2020). https://doi.org/10.3389/fcvm.2020.00025
3. Chitta, K., Álvarez, J.M., Lesnikowski, A.: Large-scale visual active learning with deep probabilistic ensembles. ArXiv **abs/1811.0** (2018)
4. Dewey, M.: The Discharge trial. (2021). https://www.dischargetrial.eu/
5. Dewey, M., et al.: Evaluation of computed tomography in patients with atypical angina or chest pain clinically referred for invasive coronary angiography: randomised controlled trial. BMJ (Online) **355** (2016). https://doi.org/10.1136/bmj.i5441
6. Filstroff, L., Sundin, I., Mikkola, P., Tiulpin, A., Kylmäoja, J., Kaski, S.: Targeted active learning for Bayesian decision-making, pp. 1–22 (2021). http://arxiv.org/abs/2106.04193
7. Föllmer, B., Schulze, K., Wald, C., Stober, S., Samek, W., Dewey, M.: Active learning with the nnUnet and sample selection with uncertainty-aware submodular mutual information measure. In: Medical Imaging with Deep Learning, pp. 480–503. PMLR (2024)
8. Gal, Y., Islam, R., Ghahramani, Z.: Deep Bayesian active learning with image data. In: Precup, D., Teh, Y.W. (eds.) Proceedings of the 34th International Conference on Machine Learning. Proceedings of Machine Learning Research, vol. 70, pp. 1183–1192. PMLR (2017). https://proceedings.mlr.press/v70/gal17a.html
9. Isensee, F., Jaeger, P.F., Kohl, S.A., Petersen, J., Maier-Hein, K.H.: nnU-Net: a self-configuring method for deep learning-based biomedical image segmentation. Nat. Methods **18**(2), 203–211 (2021). https://doi.org/10.1038/s41592-020-01008-z
10. Karanam, A., Killamsetty, K., Kokel, H., Iyer, R.: ORIENT: submodular mutual information measures for data subset selection under distribution shift. In: Koyejo, S., Mohamed, S., Agarwal, A., Belgrave, D., Cho, K., Oh, A. (eds.) Advances in Neural Information Processing Systems, vol. 35, pp. 31796–31808. Curran Associates, Inc. (2022)

11. Kaur, R., Singh, S.: A comprehensive review of object detection with deep learning. Digit. Signal Process. Rev. J. **132**, 103812 (2022). https://doi.org/10.1016/j.dsp.2022.103812
12. Kendall, A., Badrinarayanan, V., Cipolla, R.: Bayesian SegNet: model uncertainty in deep convolutional encoder-decoder architectures for scene understanding. British Machine Vision Conference 2017, BMVC 2017 (2017). https://doi.org/10.5244/c.31.57
13. Kissel, C.K., Gabus, V., Baggish, A.L.: The effects of long-term vigorous endurance exercise on the coronary arteries. Swiss Sports Exerc. Med **67**(2), 43–49 (2019)
14. Kothawade, S., Beck, N., Killamsetty, K., Iyer, R.: SIMILAR: submodular information measures based active learning in realistic scenarios. Adv. Neural Info. Process. Syst. **23**(c), 18685–18697 (2021)
15. Kothawade, S., Ghosh, S., Shekhar, S., Xiang, Y.: TALISMAN : targeted active learning for object detection with rare classes and slices using submodular mutual information
16. Kothawade, S., Savarkar, A., Iyer, V., Tamil, L., Iyer, R.: CLINICAL: targeted active learning for imbalanced medical image classification
17. Landman, B., Xu, Z., Igelsias, J., Styner, M., Langerak, T., Klein, A.: MICCAI multi-atlas labeling beyond the cranial vault–workshop and challenge. In: Proc. MICCAI Multi-Atlas Labeling Beyond Cranial Vault-Workshop Challenge, vol. 5, p. 12 (2015)
18. Nath, V., Yang, D., Landman, B.A., Xu, D., Roth, H.R.: Diminishing uncertainty within the training pool: active learning for medical image segmentation. IEEE Trans. Med. Imaging **40**(10), 2534–2547 (2021). https://doi.org/10.1109/TMI.2020.3048055
19. Pantoja-Rosero, B.G., Chassignet, A., Rezaie, A., Kozinski, M., Achanta, R., Beyer, K.: Partial annotations in active learning for semantic segmentation. Autom. Constr. **168**, 105828 (2024). https://doi.org/10.1016/j.autcon.2024.105828
20. Raff, G.L., et al.: SCCT guidelines for the interpretation and reporting of coronary computed tomographic angiography. J. Cardiov. Comput. Tomog. **3**(2), 122–136 (2009). https://doi.org/10.1016/j.jcct.2009.01.001
21. Sener, O., Savarese, S.: Active learning for convolutional neural networks: a coreset approach. In: International Conference on Learning Representations (2018). https://openreview.net/forum?id=H1aIuk-RW
22. Shit, S., et al.: clDice-a novel topology-preserving loss function for tubular structure segmentation. In: Proceedings of the IEEE/CVF Conference on Computer Vision and Pattern Recognition, pp. 16560–16569 (2021)
23. Wang, H., Jin, Q., Li, S., Liu, S., Wang, M., Song, Z.: A comprehensive survey on deep active learning in medical image analysis. Med. Image Anal. **95**(May), 103201 (2024). https://doi.org/10.1016/j.media.2024.103201
24. Yang, L., Zhang, Y., Chen, J., Zhang, S., Chen, D.Z.: Suggestive annotation: a deep active learning framework for biomedical image segmentation. Lecture Notes in Computer Science (including subseries Lecture Notes in Artificial Intelligence and Lecture Notes in Bioinformatics) **10435 LNCS**(1), 399–407 (2017). https://doi.org/10.1007/978-3-319-66179-7_46

# Applications of Human-AI Interaction, Collaboration, and Human Factor Analysis

# User Perception of Attention Visualizations: Effects on Interpretability Across Evidence-Based Medical Documents

Andrés Carvallo[1(✉)], Denis Parra[2], Peter Brusilovsky[3], Hernan Valdivieso[2], Gabriel Rada[2], Ivania Donoso[4], and Vladimir Araujo[2]

[1] CENIA – Centro Nacional de Inteligencia Artificial, Macul, Chile
afcarvallo@uc.cl
[2] Pontificia Universidad Católica de Chile, Villarrica, Chile
{dparras,hfvaldivieso,vgaraujo}@uc.cl, gabriel@rada.cl
[3] University of Pittsburgh, Pittsburgh, USA
peterb@pitt.edu
[4] KU Leuven, Leuven, Belgium
indonoso@uc.cl

**Abstract.** The attention mechanism is a core component of the Transformer architecture. Beyond improving performance, attention has been proposed as a mechanism for explainability via attention weights, which are associated with input features (e.g., tokens in a document). In this context, larger attention weights may imply more relevant features for the model's prediction. In evidence-based medicine, such explanations could support physicians' understanding and interaction with AI systems used to categorize biomedical literature. However, there is still no consensus on whether attention weights provide helpful explanations. Moreover, little research has explored how visualizing attention affects its usefulness as an explanation aid. To bridge this gap, we conducted a user study to evaluate whether attention-based explanations support users in biomedical document classification and whether there is a preferred way to visualize them. The study involved medical experts from various disciplines who classified articles based on study design (e.g., systematic reviews, broad synthesis, randomized and non-randomized trials). Our findings show that the Transformer model (XLNet) classified documents accurately; however, the attention weights were not perceived as particularly helpful for explaining the predictions. However, this perception varied significantly depending on how attention was visualized. Contrary to Munzner's principle of visual effectiveness, which favors precise encodings like bar length, users preferred more intuitive formats, such as text brightness or background color. While our results do not confirm the overall utility of attention weights for explanation, they suggest that their perceived helpfulness is influenced by how they are visually presented.

# 1 Introduction

Transformers (Vaswani et al., 2017) have achieved state-of-the-art results across a wide range of tasks, including Natural Language Processing (NLP) (Canchila et al., 2024), Computer Vision (Khan et al., 2022), and Information Retrieval (Wang et al., 2024).

Despite their success, Transformers are often criticized for their lack of interpretability. Their complex architectures, involving millions of parameters, make it difficult to understand the underlying reasoning behind their predictions

The attention mechanism (Bahdanau et al., 2014), introduced initially to enhance performance in sequence-to-sequence models, has become a central component of Transformers. Self-attention enables models to capture contextual relationships by assigning weights to input elements, such as tokens in a document. These attention weights have been proposed as a potential form of explanation for model predictions (Parra et al., 2019).

However, there is an ongoing debate about whether attention weights truly provide meaningful or trustworthy explanations (Jain and Wallace, 2019). Moreover, limited research has investigated whether certain ways of visualizing attention in text are perceived by users as more helpful.

This issue is particularly relevant in evidence-based medicine (EBM), where clinicians must quickly assess large volumes of literature to support medical decisions (Elliott et al., 2014). In such settings, AI systems must not only be accurate but also provide intuitive, trustworthy explanations that help users work more efficiently.

To address this gap, we:

1. Developed a system that classifies biomedical research articles and generates visual explanations based on attention weights from a Transformer model.
2. Conducted a user study to evaluate whether attention weights and the model's predicted probability are perceived as helpful explanations in biomedical document classification.
3. Compared different ways of visualizing attention in text and assessed whether their perceived usefulness varies depending on the type of document being reviewed.

## 2 Related Work

### 2.1 Attention as Explanation

The use of attention weights has been proposed as a means to interpret Transformer-based models (Parra et al., 2019); however, their ability to explain predictions remains debated. While some argue that attention weights do not reflect model reasoning (Jain and Wallace, 2019), others support their utility under certain conditions (Wiegreffe and Pinter, 2019). Recent studies even question the role of attention altogether, pointing instead to feed-forward layers (Geva et al., 2022). Despite this, attention visualizations remain relevant in biomedical NLP, where encoder-based models fine-tuned on domain-specific corpora can yield interpretable patterns (Roccabruna et al., 2024). Prior work in biomedical text classification has used Transformer-based models (Carvallo et al., 2020b,a; Carvallo and Parra, 2019) and investigated their robustness (Araujo et al., 2020a; Aspillaga et al., 2020; Araujo et al., 2021). In this work, we build upon these foundations to explore how attention visualization affects perceived usefulness in medical document classification.

## 2.2 Interfaces for Attention Visualization

Tools like `BertViz` (Vig, 2019) and `AttentionViz` (Yeh et al., 2023) enable users to inspect attention weights across layers and heads. However, they rarely evaluate how attention shown *within the text* affects human perception. Our study complements this line of work by conducting a user evaluation focused on perceived usefulness of attention visualizations in the text, across different types of biomedical evidence. We also build on previous applications in evidence-based medicine (Carvallo et al., 2023) and adversarial evaluation in biomedical NLP tasks (Araujo et al., 2020b) to assess how attention-based explanations perform in realistic, high-stakes settings.

## 2.3 User Studies on Explainability

User-centered XAI research indicates that the usefulness of explanations depends on user expertise, control, and context (Cai et al., 2019; Eiband et al., 2019). Recent studies highlight the importance of aligning explanation design with domain-specific needs and user profiles, especially in healthcare (E. Ihongbe et al., 2024; Kim et al., 2023). In this work, we contribute to this line of research by evaluating how medical experts perceive different visual explanations of attention and whether such visualizations support their task of classifying biomedical evidence.

## 3 The Explainable Interface

We developed an interface within the Epistemonikos[1] platform to enable interaction with a Transformer-based model that highlights word-level attention scores. Epistemonikos, a non-profit focused on evidence-based medicine, is widely used by physicians. To preserve its original workflow, we deployed our interface as a Chrome extension[2] that overlays visual explanations without modifying the underlying system.

Figure 1 shows the proposed interface with six key components: (**A**) the model's predicted study type, (**B**) a help/tutorial button, (**C**) the abstract with word-level attention highlights, (**D**) user label selection, (**E**) feedback on the predicted label and highlighted words, and (**F**) a progress bar. The interface enables the comparison of different attention visualizations, designed in accordance with the *effectiveness principle* in information visualization, which prioritizes perceptually accurate encodings of key information (Midway, 2020).

We tested three different ways of visualizing attention in text, along with a control condition without visualization, as shown in Fig. 2. In the control group (A), the abstract is shown as plain text with no visual cues. In the background color condition (B), each word's background is shaded based on its attention weight—the darker the background, the more important the word. In the word luminance condition (C), text brightness varies with attention, making relevant words appear darker. In the bar length condition (D), a horizontal bar is displayed beneath each word, proportional to its importance. In addition to attention visualization, we also tested whether displaying the

---
[1] https://www.epistemonikos.org/.
[2] https://chromewebstore.google.com/category/extensions.

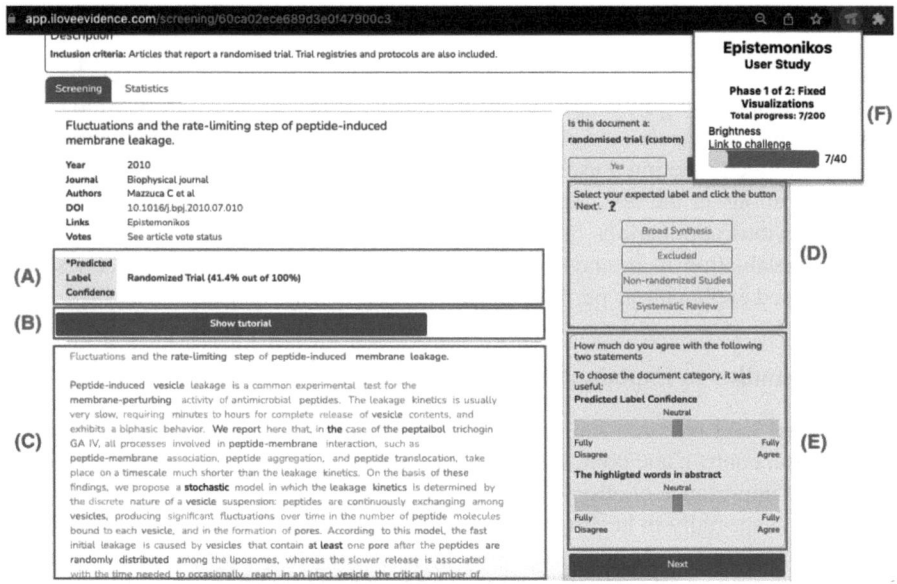

**Fig. 1.** Screenshot of the Epistemonikos user study interface used to evaluate attention-based explanations in biomedical document classification. (A) Model-predicted label and confidence score. (B) Interactive tutorial toggle. (C) Biomedical abstract with attention-based word highlighting (e.g., via brightness). (D) User Label Selection Options for Document Classification. (E) Likert-scale feedback on the perceived usefulness of the explanation components. (F) Study progress and current visualization condition.

model's predicted probability (or certainty) helped users make classification decisions. We analyzed the results across different types of evidence-based medical documents—such as randomized trials, systematic reviews, and broad syntheses—to evaluate how both attention visualization and model confidence influence users' perceived usefulness and decision-making.

## 4 Language Models

We evaluated three attention-based encoder models: BERT (Devlin et al., 2018), BioBERT (Lee et al., 2020), and XLNet (Yang et al., 2019). These models were fine-tuned for a multi-class classification task over medical literature within the context of evidence-based medicine (EBM). The classification was performed by passing the special [CLS] token through a fully-connected layer followed by a softmax activation, producing a probability distribution over five evidence types: Broad Synthesis (BS), Excluded (EXC), Randomized Controlled Trial (PS-RCT), Non-Randomized Controlled Trial (PS-NRCT), and Systematic Review (SR). SR and PS-RCT represent the highest levels in the hierarchy of medical evidence (Gopalakrishnan and Ganeshkumar, 2013).

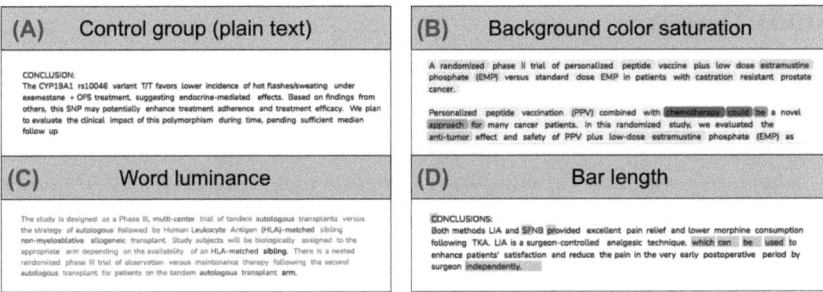

**Fig. 2.** Examples of the four ways of visualizing attention on text evaluated in the study. (A) Plain text (control condition with no attention cues), (B) background color saturation, (C) word luminance, and (D) bar length below each word.

We chose encoder-based models over large autoregressive language models (LLMs) due to their efficiency in inference, stability during fine-tuning, and direct interpretability through attention weights. Encoders are particularly suitable for classification tasks over fixed-length inputs, and their self-attention mechanisms produce structured outputs that are easier to align with human-interpretable features (Roccabruna et al., 2024).

**Table 1.** Results obtained for document classification across five biomedical evidence types. Best-performing values are in bold. The * symbol denotes statistical significance based on the Friedman ad-hoc test.

| Type | BERT | | | XLNet | | | BioBERT | | |
|---|---|---|---|---|---|---|---|---|---|
| | Prec. | Rec. | F1 | Prec. | Rec. | F1 | Prec. | Rec. | F1 |
| BS | 0.53 | 0.37 | 0.44 | **0.84** | **0.77** | **0.81** | 0.56 | 0.69 | 0.62 |
| EXC | 0.86 | 0.83 | 0.84 | **0.97** | **0.96** | **0.97** | 0.90 | 0.62 | 0.73 |
| PS-RCT | 0.63 | 0.84 | 0.72 | **0.83** | **0.89** | **0.86** | 0.64 | 0.80 | 0.71 |
| PS-NRCT | 0.91 | 0.93 | 0.92 | **0.99** | **0.99** | **0.99** | 0.82 | 0.96 | 0.88 |
| SR | 0.90 | 0.93 | 0.91 | **0.94** | **0.97** | **0.96** | **0.94** | 0.92 | 0.93 |
| **Avg** | 0.88 | 0.88 | 0.88 | **0.97*** | **0.97*** | **0.97*** | 0.85 | 0.84 | 0.84 |

Table 1 shows the performance of the three models on a large-scale EBM dataset, composed of 399,737 documents for training and 18,854 for testing, sourced from Epistemonikos. XLNet consistently outperformed BERT and BioBERT across all evidence categories, with statistically significant gains in precision, recall, and F1-score. Given its superior performance, we selected XLNet to provide attention weights for the explainable interface. These weights were extracted from the final encoder layer and averaged across attention heads to produce a word-level importance score used in visualizations.

## 5 Study Design

We designed a user study to investigate how different explanation components affect user perception during the classification of biomedical documents. Specifically, we examined three factors: *(1) whether attention-based explanations are perceived as helpful, (2) whether certain ways of visualizing attention in text are preferred or more effective, and (3) whether the model's predicted probability (or certainty) supports decision-making.*

These aspects were evaluated across multiple types of evidence-based medical articles, including systematic reviews, randomized trials, and non-randomized studies.

The study consisted of two phases:

**Phase one** was a controlled experiment in which participants used our explainable interface to classify articles. After each classification, they rated the usefulness of the model's predicted probability and the attention-highlighted words using 5-point Likert scales.

**Phase two** allowed participants to choose their preferred method of visualizing attention—or disable it entirely—and continue classifying documents under their selected setting. This phase captured user preferences in a more flexible interaction scenario.

The study involved **five medical experts from diverse specialties**, each of whom labeled 200 biomedical articles, resulting in 1,000 annotated records. The task reflected a realistic evidence-based medicine (EBM) setting, where clinicians categorize literature by study design and quality.

Attention was visualized in multiple formats, as described in Sect. 2. After each article, participants answered: (1) *On a scale from 1 to 5, how helpful was the model's predicted probability in classifying this article?* (2) *On a scale from 1 to 5, how helpful were the highlighted words in the abstract?*

## 6 Results

We analyzed the relationship between users' perceived helpfulness of model explanations both the predicted probability and the attention-based highlighted words—across different article types and visual encodings. This was done using a two-way ANOVA to explore interaction effects.

Fig. 3 shows the interaction effect between article type and visual encoding on the perceived helpfulness of *highlighted words* (i.e., attention-based explanations). Overall, users rated the usefulness of highlighted words relatively low, with scores peaking around 3.0 on a 5-point scale.

We found a significant interaction effect indicating that the perceived helpfulness of explanations depended on both the type of article and the visual encoding used. For Systematic Reviews (SR), Background encoding was rated as more helpful (M = 2.58, SD = 1.15) than Bar encoding (M = 1.75, SD = 1.09). In Broad Synthesis (BS) articles, both Luminance (M = 2.12, SD = 1.15) and Background (M = 2.32, SD = 1.14) encodings were perceived as more helpful than Bar (M = 1.57, SD = 0.89). For

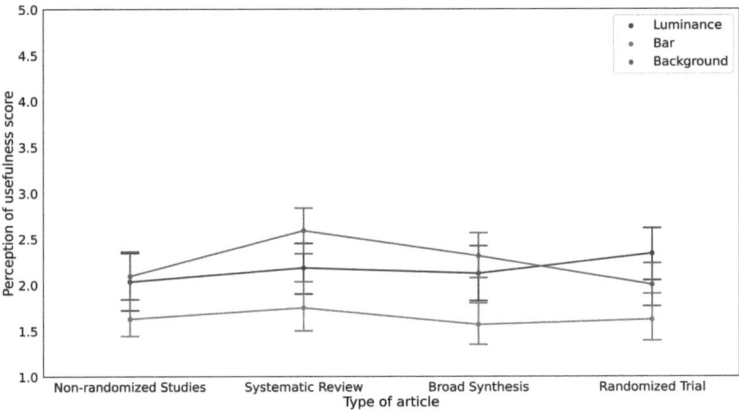

**Fig. 3.** Perceived usefulness of highlighted words by visualization type and article category. A two-way ANOVA revealed that usefulness ratings for background color and luminance varied according to the type of document, with higher ratings for Systematic Reviews and Broad Syntheses. In contrast, the bar encoding was consistently perceived as less useful across all types.

Randomized Controlled Trials (PS-RCT), Luminance encoding (M = 2.34, SD = 1.14) was also rated significantly higher than Bar (M = 1.62, SD = 1.04). Similarly, in Non-Randomized Controlled Trials (PS-NRCT), Background (M = 2.09, SD = 1.14) and Luminance (M = 2.03, SD = 1.22) encodings were rated more helpful than Bar (M = 1.63, SD = 0.82).

These results suggest that users generally found Bar Length—despite being the most perceptually accurate channel—less helpful than more intuitive encodings like Background or Luminance. This contradicts the expected effectiveness hierarchy in visualization literature.

Figure 4 presents the results of the second ANOVA, analyzing the perceived usefulness of the *model's predicted probability*. In contrast to attention-based explanations, the predicted probability was consistently rated as highly useful across all article types, with mean scores above 4.0. Importantly, we found no statistically significant differences between visual encodings (including the no-visualization condition) in terms of the perceived usefulness of predicted probabilities. This suggests that while users

**Table 2.** Mean (standard deviation) for NASA-TLX subscales across visual encoding conditions. Bolded values represent the best (lowest workload or highest performance) scores.

| Visual encoding | Mental | Physical | Temporal | Performance | Effort | Frustration |
|---|---|---|---|---|---|---|
| No visualization | 46.1 (25.15) | 25.3 (11.08) | 44.2 (23.54) | **61.6** (16.87) | 49.70 (27.32) | **27.8** (16.44) |
| Background color | **37.2** (26.81) | **24.4** (19.74) | **36.5** (26.12) | 55.3 (28.59) | **42.4** (27.73) | 30.3 (25.05) |
| Word luminance | 49.1 (30.54) | 35.1 (26.13) | 49.4 (27.51) | 50.6 (25.57) | 54.3 (30.71) | 43.3 (27.98) |
| Bar length | 48.5 (24.28) | 35.4 (22.82) | 52.5 (23.58) | 59.1 (15.58) | 56.5 (24.95) | 49.4 (21.66) |

rely on probability information, their perception of its utility is not influenced by how other explanations are visually presented. Overall, these findings indicate that attention-based explanations are more sensitive to their visual representation and the nature of the underlying content. In contrast, predicted probabilities are perceived as consistently helpful, regardless of the visual context.

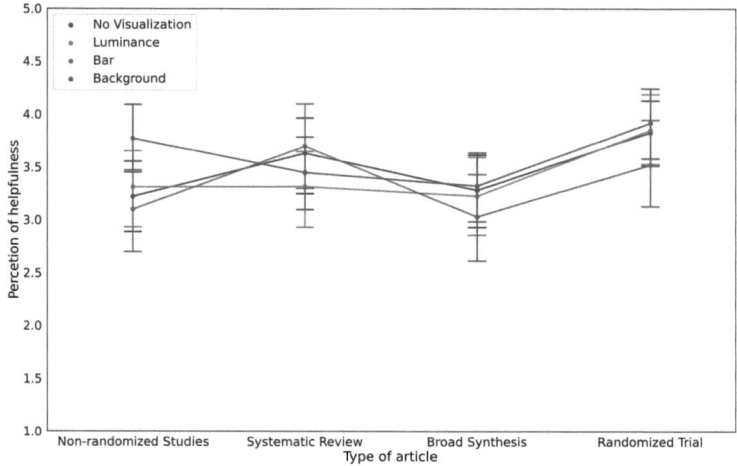

**Fig. 4.** Two-way ANOVA analyzing the interaction between article type and attention visualization on the perceived usefulness of the model's predicted probability. Results indicate that showing the model's probability is consistently perceived as helpful, regardless of the type of document being classified or how attention is visualized.

Table 2 shows the average NASA-TLX scores across different ways of visualizing attention in text. The background color condition was associated with the lowest mental demand (37.2), physical demand (24.4), temporal demand (36.5), and effort (42.4), indicating a lower overall cognitive load compared to other visualization methods. Although the no-visualization condition yielded the highest perceived performance (61.6) and the lowest frustration (27.8), it also showed higher mental demand (46.1) and temporal demand (44.2) than the background color. In contrast, bar length and word luminance produced higher scores across all workload dimensions, with bar length showing the highest frustration (49.4) and effort (56.5).

These results suggest that background color provides a favorable balance between interpretability and cognitive effort. The high performance and low frustration observed in the no-visualization condition may reflect users' familiarity with the traditional Epistemonikos interface, while more complex or unfamiliar formats appear to increase cognitive load.

## 7 Conclusions

This study evaluated whether attention-based explanations and predicted probabilities support medical experts in classifying biomedical literature. Attention weights were generally not perceived as helpful, and their usefulness varied depending on how they were visualized and on the type of document being classified. Simpler visualizations, such as background color, were preferred over more precise but cognitively demanding ones like bar length. In contrast, predicted probability was consistently perceived as helpful across all visualization settings and document types.

NASA-TLX results reinforced these findings: background color was associated with lower cognitive load, while bar length and luminance increased effort and frustration. The high performance and low frustration in the no-visualization condition likely reflect user familiarity with the standard interface for evidence-based medicine annotation.

**Limitations** include the focus on a single domain, a small sample size, and the use of one explanation mechanism.

**Future work** will explore interactive explanations and extend the study to broader user groups and medical tasks.

**Acknowledgments.** This work was supported by ANID Basal Fund, National Center for Artificial Intelligence CENIA FB210017, Millennium Science Initiative code ICN2021_004 (iHealth), Postdoctoral FONDECYT grant 3240001, and FONDECYT regular grant 1231724.

**Disclosure of Interests.** The authors declare that they have no competing interests.

# References

Araujo, V., Carvallo, A., Aspillaga, C., Thorne, C., Parra, D.: Stress test evaluation of biomedical word embeddings. arXiv preprint arXiv:2107.11652 (2021)

Araujo, V., Carvallo, A., Parra, D.; Adversarial evaluation of BERT for biomedical named entity recognition. In: Proceedings of the The Fourth Widening Natural Language Processing Workshop, pp. 79–82 (2020)

Araujo, V., Carvallo, A., Parra, D.: Adversarial evaluation of BERT for biomedical named entity recognition. In: Proceedings of the The Fourth Widening Natural Language Processing Workshop, pp. 79–82 (2020)

Aspillaga, C., Carvallo, A., Araujo, V.: Stress test evaluation of transformer-based models in natural language understanding tasks. arXiv preprint arXiv:2002.06261 (2020)

Bahdanau, D., Cho, K., Bengio, Y.: Neural machine translation by jointly learning to align and translate. arXiv preprint arXiv:1409.0473 (2014)

Cai, C.J., Jongejan, J., Holbrook, J.: The effects of example-based explanations in a machine learning interface. In: Proceedings of the 24th International Conference on Intelligent User Interfaces, pp. 258–262 2019

Canchila, S., Meneses-Eraso, C., Casanoves-Boix, J., Cortés-Pellicer, P., Castelló-Sirvent, F.: Natural language processing: an overview of models, transformers and applied practices. Comput. Sci. Inf. Syst. **00**, 31–31 (2024)

Carvallo, A., Parra, D.: Comparing word embeddings for document screening based on active learning. In: BIRNDL@ SIGIR, pp. 100–107 (2019)

Carvallo, A., Parra, D., Lobel, H., Rada, G.: A comparative dataset: bridging Covid-19 and other diseases through epistemonikos and cord-19 evidence. Data Brief **51**, 109720 (2023)

Carvallo, A., Parra, D., Lobel, H., Soto, A.: Automatic document screening of medical literature using word and text embeddings in an active learning setting. Scientometrics **125**(3), 3047–3084 (2020)

Carvallo, A., Parra, D., Rada, G., Pérez, D., Vasquez, J.I., Vergara, C.: Neural language models for text classification in evidence-based medicine. arXiv preprint arXiv:2012.00584 (2020)

Devlin, J., Chang, M.W., Lee, K. and Toutanova, K.: BERT: pre-training of deep bidirectional transformers for language understanding. arXiv preprint arXiv:1810.04805

Ihongbe, I.E., Fouad, S., Mahmoud, T.F., Rajasekaran, A., Bhatia, B.: Evaluating explainable artificial intelligence (XAI) techniques in chest radiology imaging through a human-centered lens. PLoS ONE **19**(10), e0308758 (2024)

Eiband, M., Völkel, S.T., Buschek, D., Cook, S., Hussmann, H.: When people and algorithms meet: User-reported problems in intelligent everyday applications. In: Proceedings of the 24th International Conference on Intelligent User Interfaces, pp. 96–106 (2019)

Elliott, J.H., et al.: Living systematic reviews: an emerging opportunity to narrow the evidence-practice gap. PLoS Med. **11**(2), e1001603 (2014)

Geva, M., Schuster, R., Berant, J., Levy, O.: Transformer feed-forward layers are key-value memories. In: Proceedings of the 2022 Conference on Empirical Methods in Natural Language Processing (EMNLP) (2022)

Gopalakrishnan, S., Ganeshkumar, P.: Systematic reviews and meta-analysis: understanding the best evidence in primary healthcare. J. Family Med. Primary Care **2**(1), 9 (2013)

Jain, S., Wallace, B.C.: Attention is not explanation. arXiv preprint arXiv:1902.10186 (2019)

Khan, S., Naseer, M., Hayat, M., Zamir, S.W., Khan, F.S., Shah, M.: Transformers in vision: a survey. ACM Comput. Surv. (CSUR) **54**(10s), 1–41 (2022)

Kim, D., et al.: How should the results of artificial intelligence be explained to users?-Research on consumer preferences in user-centered explainable artificial intelligence. Technol. Forecast. Soc. Chang. **188**, 122343 (2023)

Lee, J., et al.: BioBERT: a pre-trained biomedical language representation model for biomedical text mining. Bioinformatics **36**(4), 1234–1240 (2020)

Midway, S.R.: Principles of effective data visualization. Patterns **1**(9), 100141 (2020)

Parra, D., Valdivieso, H., Carvallo, A., Rada, G., Verbert, K., Schreck, T.: Analyzing the design space for visualizing neural attention in text classification. In: Proceedings of the IEEE vis workshop on vis x AI: 2nd workshop on visualization for AI explainability (VISXAI) (2019)

Roccabruna, G., Rizzoli, M. and Riccardi, G.: Will LLMS replace the encoder-only models in temporal relation classification? arXiv preprint arXiv:2410.10476 (2024)

Vaswani, A., et al.: Attention is all you need. In: Advances in Neural Information Processing Systems, pp. 5998–6008 (2017)

Vig, J.: BERTVIZ: a tool for visualizing multihead self-attention in the BERT model. Debugging Machine Learning Models. In: ICLR Workshop (2019)

Wang, J., et al.: Utilizing BERT for information retrieval: survey, applications, resources, and challenges. ACM Comput. Surv. **56**(7), 1–33 (2024)

Wiegreffe, S., Pinter, Y.: arXiv preprint arXiv:1908.04626 (2019)

Yang, Z., Dai, Z., Yang, Y., Carbonell, J., Salakhutdinov, R., Le, Q.V.: XLNet: generalized autoregressive pretraining for language understanding. In: Advances in Neural Information Processing Systems, vol. 32 (2019)

Yeh, C., Chen, Y., Aoyu, W., Chen, C., Viégas, F., Wattenberg, M.: Attentionviz: a global view of transformer attention. IEEE Trans. Visual Comput. Graphics **30**(1), 262–272 (2023)

# Simulating Inter-observer Variability Across Clinical Experience Levels for Brain Tumour Segmentation

Haley Gillett[1,2,3,4](✉), Emma A. M. Stanley[1,2,3,4], Raissa Souza[2,3,4], Matthias Wilms[5], and Nils D. Forkert[2,3,4]

[1] Biomedical Engineering Graduate Program, University of Calgary, Calgary, Canada
[2] Department of Radiology, University of Calgary, Calgary, Canada
[3] Hotchkiss Brain Institute, University of Calgary, Calgary, Canada
[4] Alberta Children's Hospital Research Institute, University of Calgary, Calgary, Canada
haley.gillett@ucalgary.ca
[5] Department of Radiology, University of Michigan, Ann Arbor, USA

**Abstract.** Human-AI collaboration is essential for the development of trustworthy deep learning (DL) models for medical image analysis. However, datasets annotated by multiple clinical experts can introduce inter-observer variability, which can then give rise to annotator biases that may be learned by the DL model. Assessment of these biases is often hindered by the limited availability of multi-observer annotations for the same datasets. To address this limitation, we present a novel simulation framework that generates realistic variations in annotated segmentations to mimic inter-observer differences across simulated human experts with varying experience levels. Using brain tumour segmentation as a representative case study, we simulated three observer labels to train DL models. Our results show that DL models learn observer-specific annotation styles. For example, models trained on the data from a simulated senior radiologist with a tendency to under-segment the tumour tissue achieved higher performance than those trained on over-segmented ones. Inter-observer agreement was not strictly correlated with experience levels nor downstream DL model performance, demonstrating the complexity of annotation biases. Additionally, datasets with single ground-truth labels may mask important differences from learned annotation bias and over- or underestimate model performance. Human-AI collaboration, although necessary for medical imaging tasks, can introduce biases that negatively affect model segmentation performance and may undermine fairness, trust, and transparency. Our study takes an essential step toward understanding these risks and provides insights that support the development of humanAI collaborative systems designed for real-world clinical applicability.

**Keywords:** Medical Image Segmentation · Annotator Bias · Human Factors · Label Noise · Inter-observer Variability · Human-AI Collaboration

# 1 Introduction

Medical image segmentation tasks that leverage supervised deep learning (DL) techniques require access to high-quality and representative annotated datasets [14]. In practice, most large-scale datasets provide only a single ground-truth segmentation label per individual, which are typically derived from multiple human observers [13]. Because these labels originate from human annotators, they are inherently susceptible to label noise, particularly due to inter-observer variability [4]. In the context of segmentation, inter-observer variability refers to differences in the delineation of anatomical regions by multiple experts [11]. Such variations are often a result of differences in expertise, interpretation, and subjective judgment about tissue boundaries [11], and are referred to here as 'annotator bias'. Inter-observer variations may also occur due to technical factors inherent in medical imaging data such as image artifacts (*i.e.*, partial-volume effects, motion artifacts, *etc.*), scanner quality, technician experience, and ambiguous or inconsistent segmentation guidelines [12]. Subjectivity in the labeling task can also introduce systematic biases into the training data. For example, patients scanned at institutions with older imaging technology or less standardized protocols may lead to less consistent segmentations. Annotator biases may be inadvertently learned by DL models and result in representations of the ground-truth that disproportionately reflect the labeling behaviors of a few annotators [12]. For instance, Takeda et al. [7] found that DL models trained using annotations from different radiologists exhibited considerable performance variability. Although inter-observer variability poses a considerable risk to the reliability of downstream DL segmentation models in clinical applications, its impact remains under-explored in the current literature.

One approach to tackle this problem is to evaluate agreement metrics across multiple observers prior to model training [8]. This approach can be used to validate the ground-truth segmentation quality by assuming that high inter-observer agreement indicates high-quality labels [18]. Some commonly proposed metrics to quantify agreement include Fliess' kappa, common agreement heatmaps, the Dice similarity coefficient (DSC), or the Hausdorff distance (HD) [18]. However, such agreement analyses cannot be assessed when only a single ground-truth segmentation is available for each image. This is common in medical imaging datasets, where producing even a single ground-truth segmentation is already resource-intensive. Additionally, high inter-observer agreement may not necessarily be an indicator of good segmentation quality. Instead, it could reflect shared biases or similar annotation behavior among observers [16].

Another approach to mitigate inter-observer variability before model training is using consensus-based methods, which combine multiple observer segmentations to generate a unified ground-truth for model training [1]. Examples of these strategies are majority vote metrics and Simultaneous Truth and Performance Level Estimation (STAPLE) [18]. Although these strategies can lead to a reasonable balance between observer preferences when generating a common ground-truth, their effectiveness depends on the assumption that inter-observer agreement is consistently high [3]. In real-world settings, it is unlikely that this assumption will hold true, as even expert annotators show inconsistencies in labeling tasks [12]. Another challenge is that by reducing multiple segmentations into a single ground-truth, one can no longer assess the extent of inter-observer variability, which may hold important insights into individual annotator behavior [3]. Furthermore, training DL models on these aggregated segmentations may yield less reliable results then if trained on individual or multi-observer inputs [3].

The presence of inter-observer segmentation variability raises critical questions about the reliability of training data, the validity of current inter-observer variability mitigation approaches (*e.g.*, agreement metrics, STAPLE, and majority vote), and the downstream impact on segmentation model performance in real-world scenarios. As a result, there is a pressing need for a highly controllable framework with known ground-truth segmentations and inter-observer differences. To address this gap, we propose a novel simulation framework that models inter-observer variability by realistically mimicking human annotation behaviors across different experience levels. This simulation framework enables the precise and automated study of human factors in DL development without requiring costly dataset segmentation by multiple annotators. In this initial proof-of-concept analysis, we apply our proposed framework to model variability in brain tumour segmentation labels using the BraTS meningioma 2023 dataset [10]. BraTS represents an ideal use case for our simulation due to its widespread use in benchmarking DL segmentation models [10], providing a meaningful and standardized baseline. This type of analysis is especially relevant for collaborative systems between humans and AI, where variability in human input can affect model behavior, trust, and fairness. By modeling this variability, our framework provides an analysis tool for the development of DL models that are more robust, interpretable, and aligned with real-world clinical workflows.

## 2 Material and Methods

### 2.1 Dataset

For the initial development and analysis of our proposed simulation framework, we used the Brain Tumour Segmentation 2023 Meningioma challenge (BraTS-MEN) dataset [10]. This challenge contains data from 1000 patients with multi-parametric magnetic resonance images (MRI) consisting of T1-weighted, T1-weighted after contrast agent application, T2-weighted, and T2-weighted FLAIR MRI sequences for each patient. Additionally, multi-label segmentation masks are available for each patient with labels of 1 = Necrotic and Non-Enhancing Tumour Core, 2 = Edema, and 4 = Enhancing Tumour [10]. The MRI data was preprocessed by the challenge organizers. Briefly described, the preprocessing steps consisted of co-registration to the SRI24 atlas space (including uniform 1 mm$^3$ isotropic resampling), and automatic skull stripping using a deep convolutional neural network [10] (Fig 1).

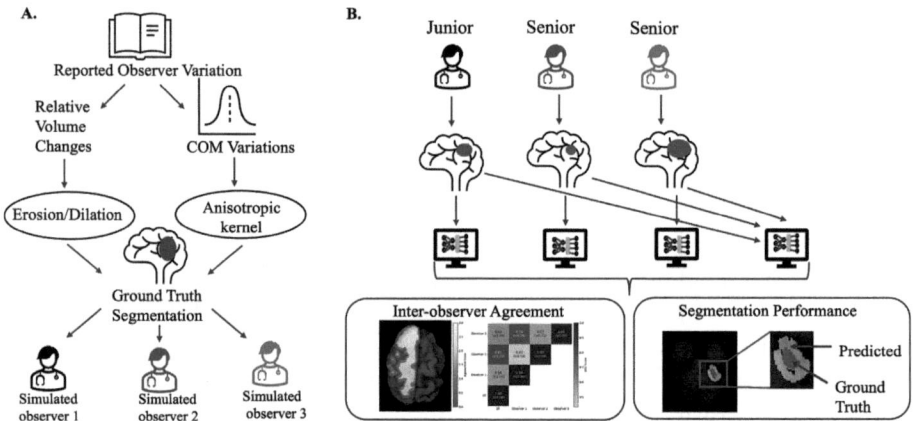

**Fig. 1.** A) Outline of experimental design to simulate three radiologist observers based on literature reported segmentation variability across clinical experience levels. B) Three observers representing junior and senior radiologists are simulated to study the effects of human factors on DL model performance using inter-observer variability and segmentation performance metrics.

### 2.2 Observer Simulation Framework

To simulate inter-observer variability in brain tumour segmentation, we modeled radiologists with varying experience levels. Inter-observer variability patterns were informed by tumour volume and mean center-of-mass (COM) differences reported by Weltens et al. [17], based on segmentations from three radiologists across four patients. These variations were introduced through controlled, realistic perturbations in both volume and spatial positioning. More precisely, volume changes were achieved using morphological operations to simulate over- or under-segmentation patterns. Spatial differences were introduced by modifying the shape of the morphological kernel using anisotropic ellipsoids. For this work, the 1000 ground-truth multi-label segmentations from BraTS-MEN [10] were binarized as background (0) and tumour (1, 2, 4), and used to generate three synthetic observer segmentations. Our simulated observer 1 mimics a junior physician with a tendency to under-segment the tumour, and serves as a middle ground between our two simulated senior segmentation styles. The simulated observers 2 and 3 represent senior physicians with tendencies to over- and under-segment the tumour, respectively.

For both tumour volume and COM variation metrics, we created relative variation factors by applying z-score normalization across all values for the observers and patients reported in Weltens et al. [17]. Volume variations, reported for each observer across four patients, resulted in four relative volume values per observer. Spatial variation, reported as mean COM deviations in three directions, leftright (LR), anteriorposterior (AP), and craniocaudal (CC), resulted in four normalized COM variation vectors.

Inter-observer volume variations were then simulated in three steps: First, each observer was randomly assigned a patient-specific volume variation factor, indexed as $i$, corresponding to one of the four patients in the Weltens et al. [17] dataset. Second, this factor was multiplied by the ground-truth volume to define a new target volume. Third, this target volume was generated by globally applying dilation, in cases where volume increased due to over-segmentation (initial volume<target volume), or erosion, in cases of decreased segmentation volumes due to under-segmentation (initial volume > target volume).

Inter-observer spatial variations were simulated using four steps: First, four sets of Gaussian distributions were modeled, one set for each patient in the Weltens et al. [17] dataset, each containing distributions for the AP, LR, and CC directions. Distributions were centered on the relative mean COM variation vectors, with a standard deviation of 0.5 voxels, consistent with the voxel-scale perturbations described by Lê et al. [5]. Second, one of the four sets of Gaussian distributions was selected based on the patient index $i$, as determined in the volume variation step. Third, for each observer and patient, values were sampled from each directional distribution (AP, LR, CC) using a half-normal approach, above the mean for over-segmentation and below the mean for under-segmentation. Fourth, these sampled values were used as the radii to construct custom anisotropic ellipsoid kernels, unique to each observerpatient pair. These ellipsoid kernels then guided the direction and shape of morphological operations, ensuring that spatial perturbations aligned with clinically observed COM variation patterns.

Finally, to ensure anatomical plausibility, all simulated segmentations were constrained using a brain mask as provided by the BraTS challenge [10]. Any morphological changes extending beyond the brain region were excluded, which ensured that all synthetic segmentations remained within anatomical boundaries.

### 2.3 Inter-observer Agreement Analysis

To assess inter-observer variability in our newly simulated dataset of 1000 patients, we employed both quantitative and qualitative evaluation metrics. These metrics can be used to estimate the level of agreement between our simulated human annotators prior to DL model training and can be used to explore the relation of inter-observer agreement and segmentation quality. To evaluate inter-observer label agreement, we used DSC scores, which quantify differences in spatial overlap [18]. For qualitative assessment, we generated standard agreement heatmaps for each patient, by combining the three observer masks [13].

### 2.4 DL Segmentation Performance

To evaluate how differences in observer characteristics influence model performance, we trained four separate DL models using the winning BraTS-MEN segmentation algorithm [2], which is based on the nnU-Net architecture. More precisely, three models were trained individually on segmentations from each of the three simulated radiologist observers. A fourth model was then trained using the segmentation masks from all three observers (*i.e.*, three masks per patient). All models were trained on the entire multi-modal dataset (4 images per patient = 4,000 images) using 5-fold cross-validation. Segmentation performance was evaluated using two standard BraTS segmentation challenge metrics [6]: DSC, where higher values indicate more accurate spatial overlap in segmentations, and 95th percentile HD (HD95), which quantifies differences in segmentation boundaries with lower values indicating greater accuracy [13]. For each model, two sets of DSC and HD95 scores were computed: one comparing the model predictions to the original BraTS-MEN ground-truth, and the other comparing predictions between the corresponding simulated observer segmentations. Both metrics allow for the assessment of how observer-specific annotation styles affect model accuracy.

## 3 Results

### 3.1 Observer Simulation Framework

When compared to ground-truth masks, the results show that our framework successfully mimics radiologists with different experience levels as illustrated by the under- and over-segmentation in Fig. 2.

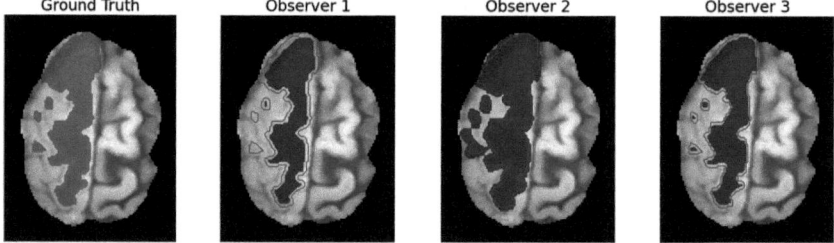

**Fig. 2.** Selected real ground-truth segmentation with variation in (synthetic) segmentation masks created with the proposed simulation framework for three observers shown with the outlined ground-truth segmentation contour in red. (Color figure online)

### 3.2 Inter-observer Agreement Analysis

Figure 3(A) shows an example of the common agreement heatmap between the three simulated annotators. Figure 3(B) visualizes DSC inter-observer and ground-truth agreement. Observer 1 (junior) shows the lowest average DSC and observer 2 (senior 1) shows the highest, against the ground-truth. For agreement between observers, observers 1 and 2 (junior *vs.* senior 1) show the lowest DSC agreement scores, and observers 1 and 3 (junior *vs.* senior 2) show the highest DSC agreement scores.

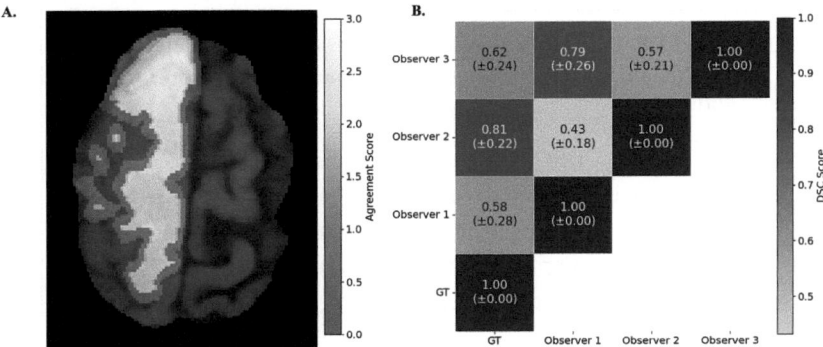

**Fig. 3.** A) Common agreement heatmap for a chosen patient in our simulated dataset. B) Inter-observer agreement in simulated dataset using DSC with standard deviation across cross-validation folds.

### 3.3 DL Segmentation Performance

Table 3 summarizes performance of the segmentation models. Among the models, the relative difference between DSC evaluated on simulated observer versus ground-truth segmentations remained relatively small (within 5%). Model 1 was trained on data from observer 1, the simulated junior radiologist, and had higher DSC when evaluated on the observer 1 segmentations compared to the ground-truth segmentations. Moreover, both evaluations had high HD95, suggesting that the model's segmentation predictions were more similar to observer 1's annotation style than the ground-truth. Thus, we can infer that the model learned observer 1 labeling tendencies. Model 2 and Model 3, trained on the data from observers 2 and 3, the simulated senior observers, achieved higher DSC when evaluated on the ground-truth segmentations than the observers' segmentations. However, the results of these models also showed high HD95 values when evaluated against both sets of segmentations. The DSC results suggest that the model may not have learned labeling tendencies related to spatial overlap, while the high HD95 values suggest that the models may have learned observer-specific boundary differences. Model 4, trained on data from all observers, showed the most consistent DSC results comparing the observer and ground-truth segmentations, and the lowest HD95 values against both segmentations. This suggests that the model learned more generalized annotator styles not related to specific observers. When comparing the four models, the highest DSC considering both segmentations was found for Model 2 followed by Model 4. The best performance in HD95 values was found for Model 4. The worst performing models measured by DSC and HD95 were Models 1 and 3, these results are aligned with our model-specific findings (Table 1).

**Table 1.** DSC and HD95 model performance validation metrics against ground-truth (GT) and simulated observer-specific (Obs) segmentations with standard deviation across cross-validation folds.

| Model | DSC (Obs) | DSC (GT) | HD95 (Obs) [mm] | HD95 (GT) [mm] |
|---|---|---|---|---|
| 1 | 0.609 ± 0.031 | 0.569 ± 0.026 | 29.17 ± 3.96 | 29.90 ± 3.96 |
| 2 | 0.656 ± 0.011 | 0.712 ± 0.026 | 20.39 ± 3.97 | 18.41 ± 3.83 |
| 3 | 0.520 ± 0.015 | 0.572 ± 0.017 | 30.04 ± 2.85 | 26.82 ± 4.62 |
| 4 | 0.621 ± 0.012 | 0.659 ± 0.005 | 10.07 ± 2.13 | 10.68 ± 2.20 |

## 4 Discussion and Conclusions

In this work, we present a novel simulation framework that models realistic inter-observer segmentation variability of human annotators. Applied to a meningioma dataset as a first proof-of-concept, our simulation imitates real-world annotation behavior with varying levels of agreement. The simulated volume variability (factor of 0.6-1.5) aligns with previously reported ranges in the literature: for example, Rasch et al. [9] observed variation factors of 1.26.1 in head and neck tumours, with reduced variability in brain tumours due to skull encapsulation, consistent with the lower factors of 0.72.0 reported by Weltens et al. [17].

Agreement scores between simulated observers did not reliably translate to downstream model performance, as demonstrated by discrepancies between inter-observer agreement and DL segmentation outcomes for observers 1 and 3. This finding highlights that experience alone does not dictate agreement levels, and that such measures may mask underlying annotator bias. In contrast, DL segmentation performance results for training on multi-observer segmentation data are supportive of previous findings that observer diversity can regularize learning and mitigate annotator bias [12]. HD95 performance results highlight that boundary errors can persist even when overall volume overlap appears similar. Although such discrepancies may seem minor, they can have disproportionate clinical consequences, particularly in applications like treatment planning, where spatial precision is critical [15]. For example, underestimating tumour boundaries may result in inadequate treatment coverage and increased risk of recurrence, while overestimation could expose healthy tissue to unnecessary treatment, negatively impacting patient quality of life [13]. Interestingly, although HD95 values showed considerable variation when models were evaluated against the ground-truth, these differences were minimal when models were compared against their respective simulated observer segmentations. This highlights the risk of using single-observer ground-truth segmentations for evaluation of DL model performance, as DSC and HD95 may misleadingly suggest similar model performance despite underlying annotator biases.

Overall, our findings suggest that individual annotation styles, rather than general attributes such as experience level, drive differences in observer agreement and segmentation performance with particular sensitivity to learning boundary differences. Our results also suggest that model performance metrics, such as DSC and HD95, may not be reliable measures of DL model success if only a single ground-truth segmentation is available. This highlights the risks of deploying models in humanAI collaborative settings without first evaluating or understanding the influence of inter-observer segmentation variability on model behavior. As such systems become more integrated into clinical workflows, developing methods such as ours to identify and mitigate human biases is essential. While our simulation framework captures key aspects of inter-observer variability, it has several limitations. One such limitation is the use of DSC as a primary evaluation metric, which is known to be sensitive to small-volume segmentations [18]. Furthermore, our simulation is based on values reported in one study, which may restrict generalizability and reflect biases from that study. Additionally, the current framework does not yet incorporate other important human factors beyond annotator experience level. Future work will expand this framework to include specialty-based differences, intra-observer variability, and more complex annotation behaviors. Human-in-the-loop systems, which acquire human input dynamically, may be especially susceptible to such biases and require further investigation into the impacts of annotator bias in real-time.

**Acknowledgments.** The authors acknowledge support from the Natural Science and Engineering Research Council of Canada and the Canada Research Chairs Program.

**Disclosure of Interests.** The authors have no relevant competing interests to declare.

# References

1. Hammond, M.E.H., Stehlik, J., Drakos, S.G., Kfoury, A.G.: Bias in medicine: lessons learned and mitigation strategies. JACC Basic Transl. Sci. **6**(1), 78 (2021). https://doi.org/10.1016/j.jacbts.2020.07.012
2. Isensee, F., Jaeger, P.F., Kohl, S.A.A., Petersen, J., Maier-Hein, K.H.: NNU-Net: a self-configuring method for deep learning-based biomedical image segmentation. Nat. Methods **18**(2), 203–211 (2021). https://doi.org/10.1038/s41592-020-01008-z
3. Jungo, A., et al.: On the effect of inter-observer variability for a reliable estimation of uncertainty of medical image segmentation. In: Frangi, A.F., Schnabel, J.A., Davatzikos, C., Alberola-López, C., Fichtinger, G. (eds.) MICCAI 2018. LNCS, vol. 11070, pp. 682–690. Springer, Cham (2018). https://doi.org/10.1007/978-3-030-00928-1_77
4. Karimi, D., Dou, H., Warfield, S.K., Gholipour, A.: Deep learning with noisy labels: exploring techniques and remedies in medical image analysis. Med. Image Anal. **65**, 101759 (2020). https://doi.org/10.1016/j.media.2020.101759

5. Lê, M., et al.: Sampling image segmentations for uncertainty quantification. Med. Image Anal. **34**, 42–56 (2016). https://doi.org/10.1016/j.media.2016.04.005
6. Menze, B.H., et al.: The multimodal brain tumor image segmentation benchmark (brats). IEEE Trans. Med. Imaging **34**(10), 1993–2024 (2015). https://doi.org/10.1109/TMI.2014.2377694
7. Nomura, Y., et al.: Performance changes due to differences among annotating radiologists for training data in computerized lesion detection. Int. J. Comput. Assist. Radiol. Surg. **19**(8), 1527–1536 (2024). https://doi.org/10.1007/s11548-024-03136-9
8. Quinn, L., et al.: Interobserver variability studies in diagnostic imaging: a methodological systematic review. Br. J. Radiol. **96**(1148), 20220972 (2023). https://doi.org/10.1259/bjr.20220972
9. Rasch, C., Barillot, I., Remeijer, P., Touw, A., van Herk, M., Lebesqué, J.V.: Definition of the prostate in CT and MRI: a multi-observer study. Int. J. Radiat. Oncol. Biol. Phys. **43**(1), 57–66 (1999). https://doi.org/10.1016/S0360-3016(98)00351-4
10. Sage bionetworks: Brats 2023 challenge. https://www.synapse.org/Synapse:syn51156910/wiki/622353. Accessed 3 Apr 2025
11. ScienceDirect: Tumor segmentation – an overview — sciencedirect topics. https://www.sciencedirect.com/topics/computer-science/tumor-segmentation. Accessed 3 Apr 2025
12. Sylolypavan, A., Sleeman, D., Wu, H., Sim, M.: The impact of inconsistent human annotations on AI-driven clinical decision making. NPJ Digit. Med. **6**(1), 1–13 (2023). https://doi.org/10.1038/s41746-023-00773-3
13. Taha, A.A., Hanbury, A.: Metrics for evaluating 3D medical image segmentation: analysis, selection, and tool. BMC Med. Imaging **15**(1), 29 (2015). https://doi.org/10.1186/s12880-015-0068-x
14. Ullah, F., et al.: Brain tumor segmentation from MRI images using handcrafted convolutional neural network. Diagnostics **13**(16), 2650 (2023). https://doi.org/10.3390/diagnostics13162650
15. Vinod, S.K., Jameson, M.G., Min, M.Y., Holloway, L.C.: Variability of contouring organs at risk in radiation therapy: a systematic review. Radiother. Oncol. **121**(2), 169–179 (2016). https://doi.org/10.1016/j.radonc.2016.08.012
16. Warfield, S.K., Zou, K.H., Wells, W.M.: Validation of image segmentation by estimating rater bias and variance. Philos. Trans. R. Soc. A Math. Phys. Eng. Sci. **366**(1874), 2361–2375 (2008). https://doi.org/10.1098/rsta.2008.0033
17. Weltens, C., et al.: Interobserver variations in gross tumor volume delineation of brain tumors on computed tomography and impact of magnetic resonance imaging. Radiother. Oncol. **60**(1), 49–59 (2001). https://doi.org/10.1016/S0167-8140(01)00371-1
18. Yang, F., et al.: Assessing inter-annotator agreement for medical image segmentation. IEEE Access **11**, 21300–21312 (2023). https://doi.org/10.1109/ACCESS.2023.3249759

# Boosting Transparency, Interpretability, and Risk Management

# Perceptual Evaluation of GANs and Diffusion Models for Generating X-Rays

Gregory Schuit[1,2,3], Denis Parra[1,2,3(✉)], and Cecilia Besa[1,2]

[1] Pontificia Universidad Católica de Chile, Macul, Chile
{gkschuit,cbesa}@uc.cl
[2] iHealth - Instituto Milenio en Ingeniería e Inteligencia Artificial para la Salud, Macul, Chile
[3] CENIA Centro Nacional de Inteligencia Artificial, Macul, Chile
dparras@uc.cl

**Abstract.** Generative image models have achieved remarkable progress in both natural and medical imaging. In the medical context, these techniques offer a potential solution to data scarcity-especially for low-prevalence anomalies that impair the performance of AI?driven diagnostic and segmentation tools. However, questions remain regarding the fidelity and clinical utility of synthetic images, since poor generation quality can undermine model generalizability and trust. In this study, we evaluate the effectiveness of state-of-the-art generative models-Generative Adversarial Networks (GANs) and Diffusion Models (DMs)-for synthesizing chest X-rays conditioned on four abnormalities: Atelectasis (AT), Lung Opacity (LO), Pleural Effusion (PE), and Enlarged Cardiac Silhouette (ECS). Using a benchmark composed of real images from the MIMIC-CXR dataset and synthetic images from both GANs and DMs, we conducted a reader study with three radiologists of varied experience. Participants were asked to distinguish real from synthetic images and assess the consistency between visual features and the target abnormality. Our results show that while DMs generate more visually realistic images overall, GANs can report better accuracy for specific conditions, such as absence of ECS. We further identify visual cues radiologists use to detect synthetic images, offering insights into the perceptual gaps in current models. These findings underscore the complementary strengths of GANs and DMs and point to the need for further refinement to ensure generative models can reliably augment training datasets for AI diagnostic systems.

**Keywords:** Medical Imaging · Generative Models · Chest X-rays · Diffusion Models · GANs

## 1 Introduction

Recent advances in generative AI have led to remarkable progress in image synthesis across domains, including medical imaging. These models-particularly

Generative Adversarial Networks (GANs) [3] and Diffusion Models (DMs) [7]-have the potential to address longstanding challenges in medical AI, such as data scarcity for low-prevalence conditions and the generation of counterfactual explanations for model interpretability.

While Diffusion Models have recently surpassed GANs in image quality and are gaining popularity in chest X-ray (CXR) generation [6], their clinical reliability remains underexplored. Most existing studies evaluate these models using proxy metrics like Frechet Inception Distance (FID) [8], which do not capture radiological fidelity or diagnostic relevance. Although some works include expert feedback, they often rely on small image sets or overlook the reasons behind radiologists' judgments.

To address this gap, we conduct a human-centered evaluation comparing GAN- and DM-generated chest X-rays. We focus on four common abnormalities: Atelectasis, Lung Opacity, Pleural Effusion, and Enlarged Cardiac Silhouette. Our study involves two structured user studies with three board-certified radiologists, who assess image realism and the presence of the intended pathology. We also collect qualitative insights on the visual cues used to identify synthetic content.

Our contributions are twofold: (1) we extend prior evaluation frameworks with a detailed, anomaly-specific analysis based on expert assessments, and (2) we offer a direct comparison between two state-of-the-art generative models, revealing trade-offs in realism versus conditional accuracy. Our findings highlight the complementary strengths of GANs and DMs and underscore the importance of human-in-the-loop validation in medical image synthesis.

To foster reproducibility, we release the source code[1], labeling interface, and generated dataset. This work aims to guide future development of trustworthy generative models for medical imaging applications.

## 2 Related Work

Generative models for medical imaging-especially GANs [3] and Diffusion Models (DMs) [7]-have shown promising results. GANs train through adversarial feedback between a generator and a discriminator, while DMs iteratively denoise random noise into images, achieving high fidelity but often at greater computational cost [2].

In synthetic medical image evaluation, Segal et al. [8] introduced a dual approach using FID scores and expert radiologist assessments. Their findings revealed that although synthetic X-rays sometimes appeared realistic, they often lacked clinical reliability. Mertes et al. [5] focused on explainability, and their user study revealed significant improvements in mental models, explanation satisfaction, trust, emotions, and self-efficacy compared to traditional saliency-based explanation methods like LIME and LRP. This work highlighted the importance of considering human factors in evaluating synthetic medical images.

---

[1] https://github.com/gregschuit/radiologist-perceptual-eval-xrays.

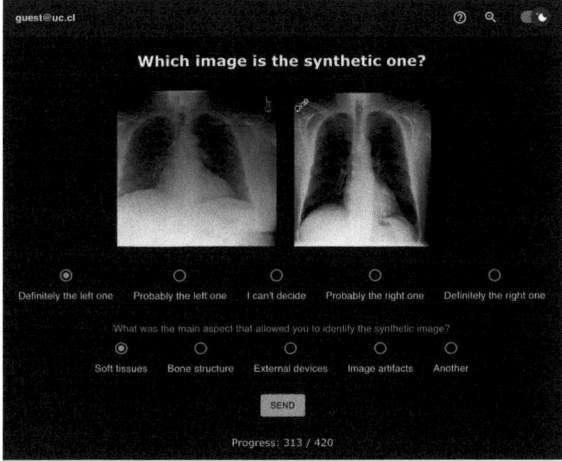

**Fig. 1.** Interface of Task 1 concerning realism. The user is asked to identify which image is synthetic when displayed side-by-side with a real one. Five possible answers are displayed to capture different levels of confidence. Also, the user should select which aspect of the image influenced their decision.

Comparative evaluations have increasingly favored DMs. Muller-Franzes et al. [6] showed that DMs outperformed GANs on multiple datasets, including CheXpert, with markedly better FID, precision, and recall. Their Medfusion study established DMs as the new standard for diverse, high-quality generation across pathologies.

Domain adaptation remains a challenge. Chambon et al. [1] addressed this by introducing RoentGen, a diffusion model fine-tuned on chest X-rays and radiology reports. They demonstrated improved image quality and representation of specific diseases, along with modest boosts in downstream task performance when using synthetic training data.

Despite progress, gaps persist. Metrics like FID lack clinical interpretability, multi-disease synthesis remains difficult, and evaluation protocols are not standardized. Moreover, few studies analyze how radiologists discern image authenticity or examine which pathologies are well represented.

Our study addresses these gaps through a dual radiologist-led evaluation of GAN and DM-generated X-rays, focusing on clinical realism, conditional accuracy, and visual patterns that inform human judgment.

## 3 Materials and Methods

As mentioned in the introduction, it is essential to obtain radiologists' evaluations to ensure the validity of our generated images. Thus, we compiled a chest X-ray dataset that included real and synthetic images. Then, we engaged a group of three radiologists in two specific tasks. The first task focused on realism: radiologists were asked to identify the synthetic image when paired with a real one

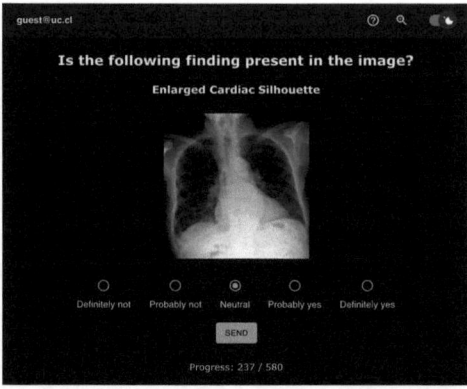

**Fig. 2.** Web interface: Task 2 concerning conditionality. The user is asked whether the given label correctly classifies the displayed image. Both real and synthetic images are evaluated. The user should answer according to a scale of five levels of agreement.

and to detail the particular features observed in each image. The second task involved assessing whether the image accurately represented the indicated condition. After that, we collected, processed, and analyzed the radiologists' labels to gauge the realism and conditional accuracy of the generated images.

### 3.1 Dataset Construction

We created a dataset of 480 PA chest X-rays: 160 real images from the MIMIC-CXR [4] along with the Chest ImaGenome Dataset [10], and 320 synthetic images (160 from a StyleGAN2 model [9] and 160 from a text-conditioned Diffusion model for chest X-rays, RoentGen [1]). The text to condition the X-ray generation on the presence of a finding was simply the name of the abnormality, e.g., *Pleural Effusion*. To condition the generation for the absence of an abnormality, the input text was *No* followed by the abnormality, e.g., *No pleural effusion*. Each image was associated with one of four abnormalities: Atelectasis (**AT**), Lung Opacity (**LO**), Pleural Effusion (**PE**), or Enlarged Cardiac Silhouette (**ECS**), marked as both present or absent. GAN images were generated with class-specific binary models; DM images were produced using RoentGen with text prompts.

### 3.2 Evaluation Tasks

Three radiologists identified as $Labeler_i$(L1: 13 yrs exp, L2: 1st-year resident, L3: 3rd-year resident) completed two tasks:

**Task 1: Realism Judgment** - Identify the synthetic image in a real-synthetic pair, with confidence level and feature-based justification (e.g., artifacts, devices). Figure 1 shows the main interface on this task.

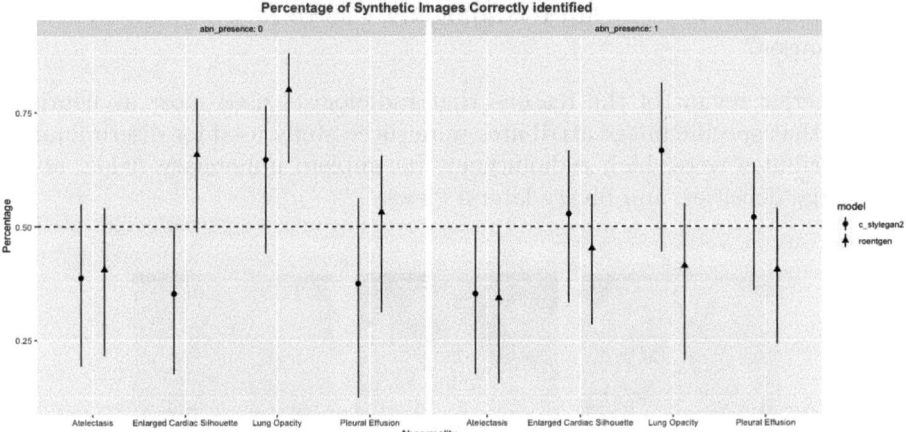

**Fig. 3.** Percentage of Synthetic Images Correctly Identified by Human Labelers. Each bar in the plot indicates the corresponding bootstrapped confidence intervals.

**Task 2: Conditionality Assessment** - Evaluate whether an image matched the abnormality label using a Likert scale, later binarized for accuracy metrics. Figure 2 shows the main interface to collect radiologists' responses on this task.

## 4 Results and Discussion

### 4.1 Are Synthetic Images Discernible from Real Ones?

In general, our results show that both models generate realistic images because most of the generated images are not discernible from real ones. We measured two metrics, Undecided Answers Rate (UAR), which indicates the proportion of cases in which the radiologists selected the neutral answer, i.e., they declared not to know which one was synthetic. Hence, higher values of UAR indicate higher model capability at realistic image generation. However, it is important to notice that lower values of UAR do not imply lower realism, as the outcome of the radiologist's decision could be wrong. We complement the analysis with the Correct Answer Rate (CAR) in those cases.

Specifically, when identifying the synthetic image, radiologists only made a decision about which image was synthetic 58.5% of the time, i.e., an UAR = 41.8%. Moreover, when a decision was made, they correctly recognized the synthetic image only 50.4% of the time. This is consistent with the hypothesis that these models generate realistic enough images that are not discernible from real ones. However, some specific cases revealed poor realism, i.e., DM conditioned on the absence of LO (CAR = 80.0%) and the absence of ECS (CAR = 65.9%), as seen in Fig. 3. As we detail next, our posterior review with radiologists pointed out some concrete visual features that revealed the image's artificial nature in these conditions.

## 4.2 What Attributes Can Radiologists Use to Distinguish Synthetic Images?

The posterior review of the reasons that radiologists used most as heuristics revealed that specific image attributes were successfully used for discrimination. Such attributes were: high radiolucency, incomplete pulmonary fields, abnormally large densities, and blurry lateral views.

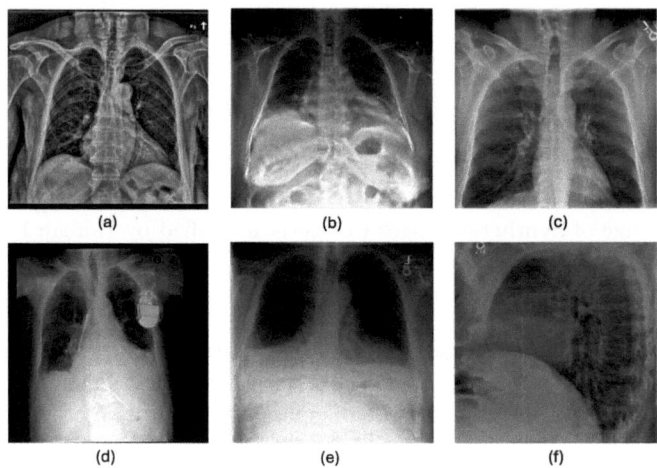

**Fig. 4.** Representative examples of labelers' heuristics: a) extreme radiolucency, b) anomalous densities in it, c) image is cut, and the lung fields cannot be observed entirely, d) real image incorrectly selected as synthetic since it had a pacemaker, e) real image incorrectly selected as synthetic because of its poor technique, f) synthetic image that was correctly identified as such because it represents a blurry lateral view.

Analyzing the visual patterns used in each case, we found that when they selected "2. Bone structure", they used **high radiolucency as an effective heuristic** when dealing with DM-generated images without ECS. This same behavior arose when they selected the reason "4. Image Artifacts."

Similarly, they correctly used **cropped image as an effective heuristic** when dealing with DM-generated images without LO. Again, this heuristic was also used for the same case when the reason was "4. Image artifacts." Further conversation with the participants revealed that an unclear definition of those reasons caused this. For example, as it can be seen in Fig. 4, a high radiolucency can be interpreted as a bone structure property because bones are highlighted with the images' contrasts, and it can also be interpreted as a general artifact of the image. The same happens with the cropped images because if the image is incomplete, it can be associated with an incomplete bone structure or as a general image artifact. Also, this last visual feature was the most common aspect when they selected the free-text "Other" option.

**Table 1.** Accuracy, True Positive Rate (Sensitivity), and True Negative Rate (Specificity) of radiologists evaluating consistency between images and labels.

|     |      | Accuracy | | | TPR | | | TNR | | | Mean Acc. | Mean TPR | Mean TNR |
|-----|------|------|------|------|------|------|------|------|------|------|------|------|------|
|     |      | L1   | L2   | L3   | L1   | L2   | L3   | L1   | L2   | L3   |      |      |      |
| AT  | real | .650 | .500 | .513 | .550 | .250 | .632 | .750 | .750 | .400 | .554 | .477 | .633 |
|     | GAN  | .561 | .659 | .585 | .250 | .300 | .650 | .857 | 1.000| .524 | .602 | .400 | .794 |
|     | DM   | .600 | .550 | .550 | .950 | .900 | .900 | .250 | .200 | .200 | .567 | .917 | .217 |
| ECS | real | .763 | .789 | .789 | .850 | .800 | .900 | .667 | .778 | .667 | .781 | .850 | .704 |
|     | GAN  | .875 | .875 | .850 | .950 | .950 | .900 | .800 | .800 | .800 | .867 | .933 | .800 |
|     | DM   | .875 | .700 | .718 | 1.000| 1.000| 1.000| .750 | .400 | .450 | .764 | 1.000| .533 |
| LO  | real | .675 | .600 | .750 | .400 | .200 | .650 | .950 | 1.000| .850 | .675 | .417 | .933 |
|     | GAN  | .553 | .553 | .474 | .056 | .111 | .056 | 1.000| .950 | .850 | .526 | .074 | .933 |
|     | DM   | .450 | .436 | .450 | .150 | .263 | .400 | .750 | .600 | .500 | .445 | .271 | .617 |
| PE  | real | .800 | .825 | .850 | .650 | .650 | .800 | .950 | 1.000| .900 | .825 | .700 | .950 |
|     | GAN  | .868 | .615 | .842 | .810 | .318 | .714 | .941 | 1.000| 1.000| .775 | .614 | .980 |
|     | DM   | .900 | .900 | .923 | .800 | .800 | .900 | 1.000| 1.000| .947 | .908 | .833 | .982 |

Another remarkable pattern in the radiologists' heuristics concerns **external devices**. Radiologists interpreted real images as synthetic when they had certain external devices, such as arthrodesis, catheters, pacemakers, and clips. **This constituted a wrong heuristic.** In the posterior review of these cases, we found that only the two less experienced radiologists followed this heuristic because they did not recognize the external devices. This suggests that participants' proper training must be ensured in future studies.

The reason **"Lung field - Cut image" was also a good heuristic**, especially when dealing with DM-generated images without LO. This pattern is important because it points to the main reason why radiologists got a higher CAR when dealing with DM-generated images without LO. This means that, when making a decision, radiologists were correct most of the time because they used this heuristic.

### 4.3 Are Generative Models Effective at Generating Conditioned Abnormalities?

The results regarding the models' ability to follow the requested conditionality were mixed. Although ECS and PE were generated with high accuracy in both models, LO and AT presented challenges, as seen in Table 1.

Specifically, results regarding the accurate generation of LO point to two gaps. The first one is the bad performance of radiologists in front of real images. Presumably, this is due to the limitations of the image format. The resolution used in the interface and during the training of GAN was $256 \times 256$ pixels, and it is very low compared to the DICOM format used by radiologists in a real diagnosis setup, which is usually above a thousand pixels square. Also, radiologists pointed out that contrast is a critical aspect that can be regulated when they inspect real radiographs, and it is also a key attribute when spotting lung opacities. This could explain why the three labelers performed badly at classifying LO within the real image set, especially in terms of TPR, i.e., in the cases where the abnormality was supposed to be present. Moreover, we see high values of TNR. This reflects a tendency to answer that there was no LO.

However, labelers performed even worse when confronting model-generated images conditioned on LO. This brings us to the second gap: the model's lack of efficacy in generating LO. As the results show, TPR is notably lower than the TNR in a more pronounced way in the synthetic sets than in the real set. This implies that, aside from the limitation posed by radiologists tagging format-limited images, there is also a performance issue with the generative models. Although this aspect was not studied in detail, we suspect critical information for generating lung opacity contrasts may be lost during the model training process. Further investigation in this line is left as future work.

### 4.4 Are DMs Superior to GANs at Generating Chest X-Rays?

Regarding realism, no significant differences were found in most categories when comparing GAN and DM. However, the GAN-based model showed significantly superior performance when conditioned on the absence of ECS. As explored in the radiologists' heuristics analysis, this difference is mainly due to the high radiolucency present in some DM-generated images when the model is prompted with no ECS. However, the reasons behind this behavior are unclear and have not been further explored in this study.

Overall, GAN demonstrated slightly better performance regarding conditional correctness compared to the DM. This suggests that, despite the DM's advantage of accepting natural language descriptions as conditions, the GAN-based model might be more effective at generating synthetic images with precise binary conditionality. However, this is subject to the prompts used with the DM. Future work should study whether changing the prompting of a text-condition generation can improve the results for DM models observed in this study.

### 4.5 Limitations

Our findings should be interpreted with caution due to several limitations. First, the relatively small sample size impacts the statistical power and generalizability of the results. Additionally, the limited number of participants may restrict the breadth of insights derived from the data. Expanding the sample size and the participant pool in future studies could reveal significant undetected differences in the current dataset. Besides, utilizing only one prompt template for the Diffusion Model represents a limitation. The model prompts can dramatically change its behavior, and different prompting techniques could yield different image quality. Another limitation is the small size of the images used in the study ($256 \times 256$), which decreases how representative the experiment is of a clinical scenario using DICOM images.

## 5 Conclusion

Since generative AI has shown impressive results in the general domain, it is tempting to believe that it could solve crucial problems in medical imaging, like data scarcity, privacy, and explainability. In addition, DMs have gained popularity due to their ability to generate high-quality images conditioned on free text, and some studies show that DMs beat GANs in the general domain [6]. However, our results constitute evidence that contradicts these assertions in the medical domain. Specifically, our results show that the generation of realistic chest radiographs is not yet a solved problem, because there are clear situations in which these images are suboptimal and recognizable.

**Acknowledgments.** This work was supported by ANID Chile, the Millennium Science Initiative Program, code ICN2021_004 (iHealth), by Chile's National Center for Artificial Intelligence, Basal Fund code FB210017 (CENIA), and by Fondecyt Regular grant 1231724.

## References

1. Chambon, P., et al.: Roentgen: vision-language foundation model for chest x-ray generation (2022). https://doi.org/10.48550/ARXIV.2211.12737
2. Dhariwal, P., Nichol, A.: Diffusion models beat GANs on image synthesis. Adv. Neural. Inf. Process. Syst. **34**, 8780–8794 (2021)
3. Goodfellow, I., et al.: Generative adversarial networks. Commun. ACM **63**(11), 139–144 (2020)
4. Johnson, A., Pollard, T., Mark, R., Berkowitz, S., Horng, S.: Mimic-CXR database (version 2.0.0). Physionet **2**, 5 (2019)
5. Mertes, S., Huber, T., Weitz, K., Heimerl, A., André, E.: Ganterfactual-counterfactual explanations for medical non-experts using generative adversarial learning. Front. Artif. Intell. **5**, 825565 (2022)
6. Müller-Franzes, G., et al.: Diffusion probabilistic models beat GANs on medical images. arxiv 2022. arXiv preprint arXiv:2212.07501 (2022)
7. Rombach, R., Blattmann, A., Lorenz, D., Esser, P., Ommer, B.: High-resolution image synthesis with latent diffusion models. In: Proceedings of the IEEE/CVF Conference on Computer Vision and Pattern Recognition, pp. 10684–10695 (2022)
8. Segal, B., Rubin, D.M., Rubin, G., Pantanowitz, A.: Evaluating the clinical realism of synthetic chest x-rays generated using progressively growing GANs. SN Comput. Sci. **2**(4), 321 (2021)
9. Shen, Y., Zhang, Z., Yang, D., Xu, Y., Yang, C., Zhu, J.: Hammer: an efficient toolkit for training deep models (2022). https://github.com/bytedance/Hammer
10. Wu, J., et al.: Chest ImageNome dataset. Physionet (2021)

# Author Index

**A**
Araujo, Vladimir  71

**B**
Besa, Cecilia  93
Biavati, Federico  58
Borges, Pedro  13
Brusilovsky, Peter  71

**C**
Cardoso, M. Jorge  13
Carvallo, Andrés  71
Chu, Sirui  25

**D**
Dewey, Marc  58
Donoso, Ivania  71

**E**
Esmaeili, Parhom  13

**F**
Fernandez, Virginia  13
Föllmer, Bernhard  58
Forkert, Nils D.  81

**G**
Gibson, Eli  13
Gillett, Haley  81
Gomez, Catalina  25

**H**
Han, Ying  35

**I**
Ishii, Masaru  25

**J**
Jiang, Zekun  35

**K**
Kramer, Patrick  25
Ku, Yu-Chun  25

**L**
Leong, Ariel  25
Li, Kang  35
Li, Yang  47

**M**
Martin-Gomez, Alejandro  25

**O**
Ourselin, Sebastien  13

**P**
Parra, Denis  71, 93
Porras, Jose L.  25
Pu, Dan  35

**R**
Rada, Gabriel  71

**S**
Samek, Wojciech  58
Schuit, Gregory  93
Schulze, Kenrick  58
Seenivasan, Lalithkumar  25

Serafimoski, Vladimir  58
Souza, Raissa  81
Stanley, Emma A. M.  81
Stober, Sebastian  58

**T**
Tang, Mengqi  35

**U**
Unberath, Mathias  25

**V**
Valdivieso, Hernan  71

**W**
Wang, Jingge  47
Wang, Xiandi  35
Wilms, Matthias  81

**Y**
Yang, Jingyun  47
Yoon, Jeewoo  25

**Z**
Zhang, Guoqing  47
Zhang, Yizhe  3
Zou, Xinrui  25

MIX
Papier aus verantwortungsvollen Quellen
Paper from responsible sources
FSC® C105338

If you have any concerns about our products,
you can contact us on
**ProductSafety@springernature.com**

In case Publisher is established outside the EU,
the EU authorized representative is:
**Springer Nature Customer Service Center GmbH
Europaplatz 3, 69115 Heidelberg, Germany**

Printed by Libri Plureos GmbH
in Hamburg, Germany